constitution- outline politics/
the economy

ALSO BY DAVID WALDSTREICHER

Runaway America:
Benjamin Franklin, Slavery, and the American Revolution

In the Midst of Perpetual Fetes:
The Making of American Nationalism, 1776–1820

SLAVERY'S
CONSTITUTION

SLAVERY'S
CONSTITUTION

From Revolution to Ratification

———◆———

DAVID WALDSTREICHER

ⓗ *Hill and Wang*
A division of Farrar, Straus and Giroux
New York

Hill and Wang
A division of Farrar, Straus and Giroux
18 West 18th Street, New York 10011

Printed in the United States of America
Published in 2009 by Hill and Wang
First paperback edition, 2010

The Library of Congress has cataloged the hardcover edition as follows:
Waldstreicher, David.
    Slavery's constitution : from revolution to ratification / David
Waldstreicher.– 1st ed.
        p. cm.
    Includes bibliographical references and index.
    ISBN: 978-0-8090-9453-0 (hardcover : alk. paper)
        1. Slavery–Law and legislation–United States–History.   2. Slavery–Law
and legislation–England–History.   3. Slavery–United States–Legal status
of slaves in free states.   4. Constitutional history–United States.   I. Title.

KF4545.S5 W347 2009
342.7308'7–dc22

                                                                2008049094

Paperback ISBN: 978-0-8090-1650-1

Designed by Jonathan D. Lippincott

www.fsgbooks.com

     5   7   9   10   8   6   4

To
Edward Countryman

Contents

Prologue: Meaningful Silences
3

1. The Mansfieldian Moment
21

2. The Great Compromises of the Constitutional Convention
57

3. Protesting and Ratifying Slavery's Constitution
107

Epilogue: Whose Constitution? Toward Civil War
153

A Note on Sources   161
Notes   169
Acknowledgments   183
Index   185

SLAVERY'S
CONSTITUTION

Prologue: Meaningful Silences

The Constitution never mentions slavery. The word does not appear. And yet slavery is all over the document. Of its eighty-four clauses, six are directly concerned with slaves and their owners. Five others had implications for slavery that were considered and debated by the delegates to the 1787 Constitutional Convention and the citizens of the states during ratification. This is many more words, with greater implications for slavery, than contained in the Articles of Confederation, the previous, notoriously weak national charter drafted in 1776 and passed eventually by the Continental Congress. All but one of these clauses protects slavery; only one points toward a possible future power by which the institution might be ended. In growing their government, the framers and their constituents created fundamental laws that sustained human bondage.

The Constitution begins by addressing the nature and law-making powers of the national government. The U.S. Congress, which would make the laws, is to be composed of a House of

Representatives elected by the people every two years and a Senate elected by the legislatures of the states. Before congressional powers are enumerated, or the composition of the Senate even described, however, readers of the new Constitution learned that the number of representatives in the House would be tied exactly to the amount of direct taxes that the national government could requisition from the states—an especially controversial issue of the Confederation era, which stretched from 1776 to 1787. Both taxation and representation would be tied to population, but in a very particular way. "Representatives and direct Taxes," begins the third clause of Article I, Section 2, "shall be apportioned among the several States which may be included within this Union, according to their respective Numbers, which shall be determined by adding to the whole Number of free Persons, including those bound to Service for a Term of Years, and excluding Indians not taxed, three fifths of all other Persons."

All other persons: Who were they? They were not free men or women. They were not apprentices or indentured servants. They were not Indians who lived among whites and paid taxes, or those who did not. That left slaves. Three-fifths of the number of slaves in any state would count toward a state's number of congressmen, and three-fifths of them would count toward how much in taxes a state would have to pay when the Congress passed a direct tax. Africans and their descendants were not being defined as three-fifths of a person, as is sometimes said, for that would have implied that the men among them deserved three-fifths of a vote, when they had none, or had three-fifths of a person's rights before the law, when they had much less than that, usually. Rather, their presence was being acknowledged as a source of power and of wealth, *for their owners.*

Several other clauses of Article I followed from the logic of what has become known as the three-fifths clause, the origins and evolution of which will be described later in this book. For now, we need only to notice how problems of power and property raised by the definition of the Congress in Article I already had the Constitution favoring people who owned people. Once three-fifths existed as the rule of apportionment, any power given to the House of Representatives would work to the relative benefit of slaveholders and the states that had more slaves. Some considered these the most important powers of all. The first clause of Section 7 specifies that "All Bills for raising Revenue shall originate in the House of Representatives," rather than in the Senate. Raising revenue meant, in effect, taxes, and taxes had been the issue that catalyzed the Revolution itself. Putting the "popular" body in charge of raising money may have been more democratic, as far as citizens of the Republic were concerned. But it also meant that the three-fifths-of-the-slaves bonus would be felt in how money was raised, when it would be raised, and how it would be raised by the federal government. Slave owners might have to pay three-fifths more, but they would have that much more power to determine everyone's federal taxes, or whether there would ever be any at all. The three-fifths clause, in other words, gave slaveholders that much more power to regulate, or even eliminate, the three-fifths more taxes they would pay. In the new American order, taxation with representation and slavery were joined at the hip.

Clauses in the eighth section of Article I reinforced the power of the Congress as a whole to levy taxes and import and export duties, and to "regulate Commerce" between the states and with other nations. Since it was very well-known that most slaves in the United States grew staple crops which were marketed abroad, like tobacco and indigo, this meant that their owners would have the power to make sure that their particular economic interests would not be overridden by senators from states with fewer slaves.

Another clause fed slaveholder power directly by allowing the Congress to mobilize "the Militia," the state-based citizen armed forces, "to execute the Laws of the Union, suppress Insurrections and repel Invasions." African slaves had not been the only insurrectionists in eighteenth-century America, but their rebellions and the threat of them had been important. From now on any slave rebellions would be a federal matter rather than just a local or regional issue.

The next part of the first article, still laying out congressional powers but now also specifying their limits, began with as explicit an acknowledgment of slavery as the Constitution contains. Most contemporaries would have understood that it referred primarily to slavery. "The Migration or Importation of such Persons as any of the States now existing shall think proper to admit, shall not be prohibited by the Congress" for twenty years, "but a Tax or duty may be imposed on such Importation, not exceeding ten dollars for each Person." The only importation of persons that had been temporarily prohibited or taxed by the North American colonies had been the slave trade. The

Congress had been denied a power that the colonies had been denied by the Crown—the power to forbid the slave trade—but then given it back after 1808. The Congress could tax slavery, but not at a higher rate than colonial legislatures had periodically done at times when growing numbers of imported Africans seemed like a threat to whites' security.

Another clause in Section 9 explicitly forbade any "Tax or Duty . . . on Articles Exported from any State," a measure that favored exporters—a group composed disproportionately of slaveholders and the merchants who worked with them. Combined with the revenue clause that gave power to tax imports to the House of Representatives, the ban on export taxes made it obvious that slavery would not be taxed out of existence in the United States any more than it would be strangled by a restriction of the trade in slaves, at that time a largely international trade. (On the other hand, things might be different after 1808 if the three-fifths bonus could be overcome in a congressional vote ending the slave trade.)

The Constitution's shorter second article, devoted to the presidency, has one clause that builds upon the three-fifths clause and thus increases the powers of slaveholders and states with slaves. It is the provision, later much criticized, for "electors" who will meet to actually elect the president. Though the manner of choosing electors was left up to the states, their number is to be equal to the number of representatives and senators—a middle ground of sorts, but still one affected by the logic of three-fifths of the slaves, and more so when the number of representatives grew larger with population. The even shorter

Article III, setting up the federal judiciary, did not really resolve the nature and powers of the federal courts, much less their role in adjudicating the differences that slavery would, in the future, bring. That these clauses do not directly address slavery makes sense given the importance of legislative supremacy to the framers' Constitution. While the executive and judicial branches did develop into mutually regulating branches, no "checks and balances" between parts of the government were envisioned with regard to slavery.

Finally, the Constitution's fourth article, a kind of grab bag of powers given and forbidden to government, addressed or implied the problem of slavery in three of its seven clauses. In requiring each state to give "Full Faith and Credit" to the laws, official records, and courts of the other states, the Constitution made it necessary for states that did not hold slaves to recognize that other states did so legally. If a human being was property in Virginia, no Pennsylvania law could free her (unless her master had taken up permanent residency in Pennsylvania). The full-faith-and-credit doctrine appears to have been formed with property and contracts and criminal proceedings like prosecutions for theft, rather than slavery, in mind. And yet slaves were property, and fugitive (runaway) slaves were, by law, criminals who had stolen themselves. By making rules to protect property across state lines, as any federal government had to do, the framers could not help but regulate slavery. Perhaps this has something to do with why the very next clause addresses fugitives explicitly: "No Person held to Service or Labour in one State, under the laws thereof, escaping into another, shall, in

Consequence of any Law or Regulation therein, be discharged from such Service or Labour, but shall be delivered up on Claim of the Party to whom such Service or Labour may be due."

Still another clause offered the U.S. government's protection against "domestic violence" to the states as one of the basic rights of the states in the union. "Domestic" could mean many things, but in the Declaration of Independence the term "domestic insurrections" had been used to describe Britain's arming of slaves against their American masters. This new constitutional doctrine separated domestic threats from such foreign "Invasion," but the legacy remained. States joining in a stronger union raised basic issues of security as well as property and power, issues that unavoidably raised the matter of slavery, which the Declaration had brought up only as an example of British tyranny.

Because the framers' Constitution sought to govern, in other words, it sought to govern slavery. Debates over representation and taxation—the basic constitutional issues that led to the American Revolution—also led directly back to the problem of slavery. Electing a president and creating mechanisms for security led to slavery. The relationships of the states and their laws to each other implied slavery.

All this suggests a proslavery constitution, in intention and effect. And yet we have that curious silence to explain: the refusal to mention the word. There is also the twenty-year limit to the ban on anti-slave-trade legislation. If the federal constitution was fashioned by the slaveholders, for the slaveholders, why is it there? Why not ban federal interference with slavery forever? Even the three-fifths-of-the-slaves clause is open to question as a proslavery device. Sixty percent is not one hundred percent, after all. What do these contradictions, ambiguities, and silences mean?

This book is a work of narrative history. It explains the meaning of slavery in the Constitution by tracing slavery in the Revolutionary background, the Constitution's framing, and the public debate that followed. As in all works of narrative history, the interpretation builds on the order of significant events.

Narrative history, like every other mode of discussing reality, must rely on definitions of real-life phenomena, definitions that generalize and even theorize the nature of dynamic institutions like slavery and American constitutions. The importance of definitions can be seen in the ways that historians have tried to explain slavery's presence in (or presumed absence from) the Constitution.

The current scholarly consensus on the nature of the "grand federal discussion" of 1787–88 stresses the exercise of creative statecraft by well-informed political thinkers like James Madison and Alexander Hamilton. In the crucible of debate, they advanced practical, constitutional solutions to problems in republican government—government by representatives of the people. According to the historians Bernard Bailyn and Gordon S. Wood, the Constitution was a fulfillment of the American Revolution because the Revolution was itself most centrally a rebellion in favor of better, more representative government—a backlash by provincial Britons angry about threats to their traditional liberties. The Constitution culminated a realistic turn, away from the idealism, crowd actions, popular committees, and legislative activism of the Revolutionary years, toward more practical ways of ensuring the survival of the Republic on the national as well as state and local levels—such as constitution making itself. Ideology gave way to reason. The American Revolution did not explode out of unrealistic expectations, spiraling radicalism, or counterrevolution. The Constitution, which Bailyn calls the "ideological fulfillment of the American Revolution," proves that the Revolution was reasonable, its violence defensible, its limits necessary.[1]

The "republican" or "ideological" school tends to see slavery as at most a side issue—a distraction that nearly derailed the Constitution. This is true even though the same historians are sometimes willing to discuss the issue of slavery in other contexts. There are two reasons for this. One is that scholars of republicanism take ideas and rhetoric most seriously. In doing this, they have advanced our understanding of political change in this era. But they tend to see slavery as the opposite of ideas, of discussion, of reason. Slavery in their view was an ancient institution propped up by a traditional, shared, and irrational racism that, Bailyn and Wood argue, hardly anybody challenged until many decades later.

Yet recent scholarship depicts African slavery in the eighteenth century as a dynamic, changing, modern institution. Its innovations, and the rise of enlightened critiques of colonialism, contributed to the emergence of antislavery during the same decades, the 1760s and 1770s, when North American colonists challenged what they saw as innovations in imperial governance. The focus on ideas also leaves scholars in the republican school ill equipped to deal with topics that were sometimes too sensitive to discuss openly, or that the powerful had an incentive to tamp down. They dismiss as mere propaganda, for example, the tendency of British opponents of the American Revolution to use the slavery issue against the patriots. (This was the very way that earlier historians dismissed patriots' republican rhetoric before Bailyn and others rescued the provincial colonists' sincere fears of tyranny.) Instead, these historians bring slavery back into the narrative as post-Revolutionary, *American* antislavery. In a happy if unintended consequence of republican thinking, the patriots' consideration of their political oppression, which they called slavery, forces them, through an unstoppable "contagion of liberty," to begin to question African slavery, if not racism. According to the Bailyn-Wood view, this explains the Constitution's silence about slavery and suggests the praiseworthy antislavery implications of that silence. It also excuses the framers from having done anything more.[2]

Another reason that these leading historians downplay slavery has to do with the logic of republican ideology in particular. Historians, as Bailyn has said so eloquently, must try to understand and explain the worldview of their subjects.[3] Republicanism was a theory of politics that stressed the need for citizens to guard against the corruption that occurred when rulers were not answerable to the citizens. The emphasis is on the virtue of citizens, their rights and duties to resist oppression. Tyranny was inevitable; virtue, and the people, always lost in the long run—but the good fight had to be fought nevertheless. That was the story before 1776. But with the creation and survival of our own constitution, the republicanism of the Revolution became for American citizens (and their descendants down to our own day) not a story of inevitable loss, but instead one about underdogs who finally won. In such a story there is even less room for the oppressed of the (formerly) oppressed, those tyrannized by the tyrannized.

When students of the past look at the founding through republican eyes, slaves simply do not belong on the agenda. Slavery can at most appear as a "contradiction" or "paradox" to be dealt with later. Some scholars who focus on the history of political theory follow such assumptions to their logical conclusion and justify the right of eighteenth-century white republicans to exclude slaves (or women or anyone else) from the citizenry if they chose to do so. At least this view acknowledges that the founders made an active choice, rather than just passively receiving racism.[4] American revolutionaries struggled to keep the entire Western world focused on *their* potential political enslavement, rather than on their African slaves' actual bondage. As we will see, critics of the Revolutionary movement forced the issue of those enslaved Africans into the conversation about British and American rights during the 1760s in ways that the founders were still scrambling to deal with twenty-five years later. The founders' republican ideas and rhetoric properly remain a starting point in understanding the Constitution. Any interpretation of the founding fails as history, though, when it preserves the bias inherent in those ideas and rhetoric against taking slaves seriously as political subjects, or slavery seriously as a political issue.

This is where theory, or the definition of key terms, can help us to pay attention to parts of the story that might otherwise be missed. Slavery was not solely an institution for the theft and oppression of people from another continent who had darker skins. It was a variety of governance in an age when government was not merely about protecting liberties but also about power over other people and property (including people who were property). The story of the Constitution as a last stage in the development of Revolutionary republicanism is incomplete. It needs to be retold, this time with a non-republican, more realistic understanding of slavery and politics. It also requires a more holistic, less ideological, and more cultural understanding of slavery's place in politics. Succinctly, slavery was a constitutional matter. It was also controversial in an international as well as an American context. We cannot have our creative founding fathers without acknowledging their disturbingly artful contributions to the politics of slavery.

A different school of thought describes the Constitution as the result of a political struggle among economic interests, and in doing so keeps slaves in mind, at least as property. It builds on Charles Beard's landmark *Economic Interpretation of the Constitution of the United States* (1913), one of the most famous and most debated works of history in the twentieth century. Beard argued that the framers were motivated primarily by their ownership of bonds and notes issued by the state governments and Continental Congress, bonds that they had sometimes bought at depreciated values. These men had an economic interest in the creation of a stronger federal government that would assume the debts of both the Confederation and the Revolutionary state governments, preferably paying every penny of those debts. The value of these debts—and who would pay them—had already become a controversial issue. Some who had attended the Constitutional Convention had speculated in "soldier notes"—the IOUs given to soldiers in the Continental army, which were being sold by desperate, discharged soldiers for much less than their face value. (Imagine inflation that affected only paper money, not coin, so that poor people started trading in their dollar bills for dimes and quarters.) For Beard, the federal constitution was to a significant degree a reflection of certain monetary interests—those of merchants and speculators who hoarded paper, rather than ordinary farmers, who did not.

Beard exaggerated the influence of this one issue at the convention and in the states. And because slave owners were so often farmers, he tended not to separate their interests from those of other farmers. He believed that the slave owners who influenced the debates in the convention were those who were likewise holders of notes, so slavery itself was not the issue that shaped the Constitution or its ratification. But Beard's importance remains, because he was one of the first to advance an economic interpretation of why the Constitution looked the way it did and why it came to be approved by the otherwise-suspicious states.

If the Constitution can be said to have favored wealth, why

should it not have favored the great wealth of southern plantation owners? After all, slaveholding nationalists like George
Washington and James Madison guided the creation of a constitution that protected slavery. The publication in 1840 of James
Madison's notes on the Constitutional Convention helped turn
Garrisonian abolitionists toward an understanding of the Constitution as proslavery. "The Garrisonians were correct," argues
Paul Finkelman: the only mystery is what A. Leon Higginbotham Jr. called the founding slavocrats' "nondisclosure" of
their true desires.[5] More cautious versions, as in a classic essay
by Staughton Lynd, suggest a "deal" at the convention, quite
plausible if impossible to prove, between Northerners or Easterners who wanted a stronger central government to control
trade and people from the Deep South like Charles Cotesworth
Pinckney, a delegate who returned home and told the South
Carolina legislature that "considering all circumstances, we have
made the best terms for the security of this species of property it
was in our power to make."[6]

The sheer number of constitutional clauses that protect slavery certainly points in this direction. Yet in describing the
proslavery constitution as a compromise, rather than simply a
reflection of the founders' interests, the more careful neo-
Beardians also point us back toward the concerns of the republican or ideological school. There was a politics to the
compromise, expressed and captured in discussions, debates,
arguments, ideas, and rhetoric. Some things were said; others
were not. If deals were made, they were also kept secret. Both
the secrecy and the debates are part of the story.

It will be apparent by now that I am proposing a solution to the interpretive problem of slavery and the Constitution that draws on both the republican and the progressive schools—on both Bailyn and Beard. I will pay attention to slavery as an economic and political interest and as a topic of debate, in what was said and written, when, where, and why. The freshness, I hope, will be in the telling as much as in my conclusion that slavery was as important to the making of the Constitution as the Constitution was to the survival of slavery.

There is, unavoidably, a theoretical claim here, though, and it has to do with how we define slavery and constitutions. The republican school defines them as mutually exclusive, as different categories of ideas, or slavery as a matter of interest rather than of ideas. The Beardians see slaveholding as a real interest and constitutions, like all politics, as compromises of interests. Yet while the notion of compromise may explain the Constitutional Convention, it does not tell the whole story, for if the framers' compromise intended to keep slavery out of national politics, it failed miserably. Slavery, in part because of the U.S. Constitution's manner of dealing with it, became central to American national politics in the nineteenth century.

Slavery indeed was less than six degrees of separation from every major political issue in pre–Civil War America. One reason for this is that slavery was a major aspect of the American economy. The livelihoods of people in the North as well as the South depended on the products of slave labor, on import and export policies, and on the running of related services. The stronger federal government created by the Constitution had become desirable in part because of the economic vulnerability of the less united states during the 1780s. Therefore, because the Constitution had economic implications, and set the stage for a national economy, it could not avoid having implications for slavery and creating a constitutional politics of slavery.

Just as important, slavery was also a form of government over people. It defined sovereignty over individuals, as well as property in them. Like the Constitution, slavery was inherently a matter of fundamental law. It defined the places of people in their society. The Constitution denied the presence of slaves in that society because it privileged politics and representation, but it defined slaves socially even as it denied them politically. Republicanism, it might be argued, was favored by many members of the Revolutionary generation precisely because, unlike monarchy (which made all subjects under the power of the king) or democracy (which would ideally render all subjects equal under law), it upraised the political powers of a master class while retaining a place for slavery and other kinds of dependency.

But republicanism had to be worked out. Slavery retained its links to everything else in American politics not least because American politics worked through the problems and possibilities of republican government, before, during, and after 1787.

Government implied the problem of slavery. The issue of slavery was one of government. The "grand federal discussion" about rights and powers in America could not help but also be a debate about slavery, despite the framers' attempts to keep talk of slavery quiet. The American revolutionaries fled a federal, imperial government that might well have begun to regulate slavery in earnest. When they created a federal and imperial government of their own, they faced that problem all over again.

Like most people, and like most politicians, the founders wanted to have it both ways. They wanted the wealth and power that slavery and its governance brought without the moral responsibility that, it will become clear in these pages, they also knew came with slavery. Silence, compromise, and artful design characterized their solutions. The silences are not absences: they had meanings that were understood and debated. Contemporaries discussed, bargained, and agonized over slavery more than we have realized—all the more so after the Constitutional Convention, in light of the Constitution's silences. The debates and compromises over slavery played a central part in the creation of the U.S. Constitution, shaping the character and nature of the government it formed. What follows is the story of those debates and some of the people who participated in them, along with a brief consideration of the consequences.

ONE

The Mansfieldian Moment

"Rule Britannia, rule the waves," went the popular song of 1740. "Britons never will be slaves." Written at a moment when Britain was at war on the seas, battling for trade and for colonies, the song identified ordinary British people with a broader empire. Freedom came with rule overseas. Freedom *and* rule, together, exemplified the opposite of human bondage, for those who sang the song. Freedom explained itself: the opposite of slavery. Rule explained the enslavement of others in the empire.

There is not much evidence that this song was particularly beloved in British North America.[1] Its invocation of slavery may have been a bit too overt, with slaves so nearby. Certainly the emphasis on British overseas rule clashed with colonial presumptions of self-government. During the early eighteenth century the growth of the empire and the growth of slavery posed fundamental questions about freedom, governance, and national identity. The unwritten British constitution, composed of Parliament's laws and judges' interpretations, proved flexible enough to handle these questions until an expensive world war and a vast addition of North American territory raised them anew. The politics of slavery played a significant part in that imperial crisis and·in its better-known results: a revolutionary war and the creation of the United States.

In the early modern world, the British came late to empire, and still later to slavery. The Spanish had pioneered both institutions, and the British did not so much decide to enslave natives in the Americas or Africa as they found ways to get in on the system. Early idealism, whereby Englishmen imagined they would find more peaceful ways to exploit the New World's resources and compete with the rest of Europe for the balance of power on the Continent, gave way to battles for conquests and similar strategies. Rather than being between slavery and freedom, the basic difference lay between the gold-mining operations of the Spanish Empire and the agricultural model of the English, who at first had to settle for lands without precious metals. When the English gained footholds and then settled in zones like Barbados that supported cash crops like tobacco and sugar, they turned first to native laborers, then to their own poor populations, and finally to Africans in growing numbers. During the mid- to late seventeenth century, the mainland colonies of Virginia and, later, South Carolina grew rapidly on the Caribbean model. Within a few decades, the northern colonies of New England, Pennsylvania, and New York experienced their own population explosions, thanks to the opportunities to supply the southerly tobacco and sugar colonies with food, with ships, with all kinds of supplies. During the same years, more and more Africans toiled in those places.

Each colony was different—in size, in trade, in form of government, and in labor supply. Slavery was one of the institutions that exemplified these differences. Yet during the eighteenth century each prospering colony became more enmeshed in an imperial system of supply and demand operating within a competitive world often at war. The more integrated into the Atlantic system each colony became, the more slaves arrived there, on the same ships that delivered New World produce and returned Old World supplies in exchange.

Theoretically, the British Empire ran its colonies and their economies for the benefit of the mother country and, secondarily, the empire as a whole. In practice, this meant considerable autonomy for the colonists, and allowances for local customs by imperial officials. According to the folks whose parents had migrated across the ocean from various parts of the British Isles, these very freedoms were what made them English. A series of crises in late-seventeenth-century England had helped develop distinctly English ideas of traditional liberties, guarded by Parliament and a king who no longer was divinely authorized but rather was himself a guardian of parliamentary liberties. Originally, the king had been the special overseer of overseas "dominions" and used them as favors, giving away lands and trading well-paying jobs like colonial governorships for political support in Parliament. Eventually, the king ruled his dominions in consultation and cooperation with Parliament through the Board of Trade, which had the power to disallow the acts of the provincial assemblies or legislatures. The two revolutions in late-seventeenth-century England—the civil wars of 1641 to 1660 and the "glorious" overthrow of James II in 1688—tended to strengthen the parliamentary central government of England while drawing attention away from the colonies. Colonists used the opportunity to claim their own liberties and identify those claims with constitutional developments in England.

What no one wanted to face was that the claims of Parliament to extend its rule in the name of the British people could conflict with the claims of white colonists to run their own local societies in the name of their "English" rights. Occasionally, when the interests of the home country conflicted with those of some colonial leaders, a standoff occurred. Sometimes colonial officials would back down, or find a compromise. Sometimes they would decree otherwise—compelling obedience to central authority. Sometimes colonists would simply disobey, trusting distance to cover the difference between the letter of the law and its lax enforcement. British imperial government, and the fighting of its increasingly regular wars with the French and Spanish empires, was a matter of constant negotiations, and, increasingly, lobbying as well. The mainland colonies began to send informal representatives to London, as well as letters "home" on the same ships that carried their goods to distant markets.

Because of the sheer centrality of slavery in the British Empire by the mid-eighteenth century, some of the more difficult to resolve controversies between individual colonies and the home government did concern slaves and the things slaves produced. Northern mainland colonists expressed great frustration, for example, when Parliament passed the Molasses Act of 1733. This law tried to make it more difficult for British American shippers and rum distillers to trade with the French sugar-producing colonies—a trade that hurt the British West Indies. That such legislation passed Parliament showed how much more important the sugar colonies, with their highest proportion of slaves to settlers, seemed to London. The experience of losing out to the British West Indians did not cost Rhode Island and Massachusetts merchants much trade. Instead, it led them to become bolder smugglers. In Rhode Island, where governors were elected, they also learned to support men like Stephen Hopkins, who made it unofficial policy to discourage the collection of duties and the capture of illegal traders.

Colonists began to develop arguments for why freer trade, and customary liberties, suited the empire as well as the colonies. Benjamin Franklin, the owner-editor of *The Pennsylvania Gazette*, paid close attention to the efforts of Joshua Gee, a merchant and colonial lobbyist, to argue that the weavers of wool in the northern colonies were just as important to the health of the empire as the growers of sugar in Barbados. Why? Because they made the clothes that the slaves wore. Franklin also copied out a position paper written by James Logan in 1732 that equated northern colonial freedom with British imperial prosperity. Unlike the West Indies, the northern colonies occupied more territory, grew more rapidly, "and which is no Trifle in their Case, much more mildly Treat their Slaves."

In 1750, when Parliament passed the Iron Act, an attempt to

restrain the growing middle colonies' iron industry from underselling English manufacturers, Franklin took the occasion to develop an entire theory of imperial population growth, economy, and governance. More colonists in the empire peopling remote regions, producing and buying and selling according to opportunity, meant more wealth all around. It made no sense for the British to worry about the northern colonies manufacturing too much—or trading too much sugar—because prosperity in the northern colonies meant population growth, which translated directly into a larger market for English manufactured goods.

The only real threat to the system, Franklin argued, was the spread of large-scale African slavery to the northern zones. Africans, because they were property, not citizens, did not consume imports; in the long term they were not productive members of the empire. Slaves were "by nature" thieves (an argument he later clarified to read "by the nature of slavery"). Instead of forbidding colonial manufacturing, Parliament should forbid the only threat to England's manufacturers: the possibility that cheap slave labor—like the slaves being used by Pennsylvania iron makers—might undersell goods made in England. Regulate slaves and slavery, or let us do so, Franklin was arguing; but keep your hands out of the pockets of productive British citizens.[2]

Why was Franklin making this argument? One thing that is certain is that around 1748, at the end of another cycle of European conflicts that turned into wars for colonies, some British officials were beginning to advocate for a stronger, more centralized apparatus of imperial government. Simultaneously, experts on the colonies and trade displayed a keen appreciation of slavery's growth and importance. One influential member of the Board of Trade, Malachy Postlethwayt, called the "African trade" (by which he meant the trade with Africa that included slaves) "the fundamental prop and support" in the British Empire. In his analysis, as in the thinking that went into the Woolen Act and the Molasses Act, the northern colonies (and even the tobacco growers of Virginia) appeared as mere subsidiaries to the larger and more important African-Caribbean-European trading system. Northern prospects depended on imperial protection, including permission to enslave and trade. James Abercromby, another colonial official, wrote in 1752 that lucky immigrants to America became "landlords with extensive possessions," in part through the use of slave labor. All the more reason to make sure these highly privileged colonists followed the laws made in England "in all cases whatsoever."[3]

Franklin was aware of this trend in thinking about the colonies and sought to provide an alternative, particularly in the matter of increasing taxes and legislation. Maybe the northern colonies, with fewer slaves, were different. He was trying to draw a distinction between, on the one hand, the West Indies and southern plantation colonies, with their large numbers of slaves, and, on the other hand, the northern colonies like Pennsylvania. In doing this, Franklin began to play an important role in discussions of colonial governance and of slavery. It was typical of his brilliance that he so early perceived, and tried to shape, the relationship between the two institutions.

Yet the essay failed to achieve its goals. That may have been because of its counterintuitive suggestion that slaves did not actually produce wealth. Or it may have been his compensatory, over-the-top concluding appeal that Britain ought to be a "white and red" (northern European and Native American) empire at a time when its "black" and "swarthy" (African, German, and other non-English European) men and women were doing so much of the empire's work.

The essay failed to influence policy for another reason, though, one that Franklin's culminating focus on slavery and then race gave away. By 1750 the British colonists had developed a severe image problem. When people in England thought of America, they did not think of a place of British freedom, even though British people often crossed the ocean for economic and religious opportunities. They thought of a place less British, a place of unfreedom, a place with indentured servants, convict laborers also bound for a period of years, and slaves. During the same years when imperial ties and trade thickened, and colonists participated in wars that made them feel more British, negative perceptions spread, reinforced by the habit, born of interest, that some Britons had of seeing the colonies as inferior because they were unfree. Travel writers and novelists were less impressed by the color line that made slaves of only Africans and some natives, while leaving Europeans free after seven or fewer years, than by the generally pervasive practices of unfreedom on which colonial prosperity seemed to rest.

By the 1750s, writers for the press in England were increasingly likely to bring up the unfree conditions in the colonies as an example of why the colonies needed to be more tightly regulated. England's desire to assert more control occurred at a time when the British West Indies colonies were gaining power and prominence in the imperial scheme of things. This reflected an access to power that few if any North Americans possessed. Absentee planters bought English estates and gained seats in Parliament, something no North American ever did without returning to England for good.

While the continental colonists did not lack influence, when compared with the West Indian planters, they felt as if they had none: there were so many more of them than there were white West Indians. Leaders like Franklin, who in 1757 went over to London to represent the interests of Pennsylvania, saw the North American mainland as the future, even if mainland trade depended on ties to the British as well as the French Caribbean. With white colonists surging into the Ohio River valley, some English observers agreed. The next major war set the stage for change because it began not in Europe or on the high seas but near present-day Pittsburgh, over the presence of forts in Indian territory claimed by both the French and the British.

The Seven Years' War became another world war, fought in India and the Caribbean as well as in the Great Lakes and Hudson River valley. But it was won, once again, on the ocean. England took French Guadeloupe and Martinique in 1759. A transatlantic debate ensued about whether to give back those islands at the bargaining table, as England had done with former French possessions in previous wars, or to exchange them for French Canada. Franklin weighed in with an important pamphlet, again depicting the sugar islands as inferior to the vast cold northern lands. The British, surprisingly, kept Canada.

This time, the northern Americans got exactly what they wanted—the removal of the French threat to the north—in a war that had depended on their active support. (The war hardly touched the southern mainland colonies, and they largely sat out the conflict.) The Northerners had resisted the demands of British officials that they pay for the war and follow British military orders; when the pro-American William Pitt became prime minister, his winning "blue-water" strategy dictated reimbursing the colonies for their expenses and making them more equal participants in the war effort.

The colonies, however, would have to pay to play. Politically speaking, raising taxes in England, instead of in the colonies, could only be sustained temporarily. In 1760, at Pitt's urging, the home government was already ordering enforcement of the old rules against illicit trade with the French sugar islands.

New Englanders responded first. "I know not why we should blush to confess that molasses was an essential ingredient in American independence," John Adams would write years later, remembering the central role of Yankee sugar merchants in the first protests against new imperial regulations. When the governor of Massachusetts tried to enforce the Crown's right of search and seizure in 1761, remembered Adams, the lawyer James Otis argued against "writs of assistance" that allowed any British official to compel local officials to help search for illegal goods. Standing in court before the wigged representatives of the Crown, Otis created a sensation by invoking natural rights and traditional British privileges against British authority. He called all such regulations going back to the Navigation Acts of a century before "instruments of slavery" and unconstitutional.[4]

What was Otis talking about? Like most lawyers preaching to a judge and jury, he was trying to persuade, pushing logic a bit further, but not so far that it would fail to make sense. To be British in the age of empire meant never being a slave. It meant having an interest in the empire; it meant having rights to pursue economic interests, to have property. If rum was "the life blood of colonial commerce," nothing could be more threatening to traditional British rights than interference with the rum trade. To be British, indeed, meant to translate economic interests like trade into questions of rights, liberties, and fundamental law. And economic interests, in New England as well as in Virginia, included slaves and the things slaves made.[5]

In these ways, American slavery and the imperial controversy were joined at birth, never to be separated. There is no other way to explain how quickly slavery emerged as a central topic, and as a kind of rhetorical sledgehammer, in the debate over colonial rights. Many historians insist that the use of the word "slavery" to refer to taxes or restrictions of liberty simply came to seem hypocritical in light of racial slavery. It certainly did eventually, but this emphasis neglects the more basic, original link of British rights to property, the fact that slaves were property, and that both slavery and property were intrinsic to what colonies were all about: agricultural production and trade.

That link became only more apparent when the Seven Years' War ended and a new ministry in London sent its fastest ships to enforce the old Molasses Act. Meanwhile, rumors emerged of a coming act of Parliament setting new taxes, an American Revenue Act (1764) that became known as the Sugar Act because it focused especially on the most lucrative and most-often-smuggled goods in colonial trade.

Again New Englanders swung into action. It helped that on this occasion they could blame the British West Indians, who had supported a crackdown against trade with rival sugar islands, rather than the home government itself. Rhode Island's governor, Stephen Hopkins, explained that all of New England's trade with the Caribbean and Africa, which included important supplies of slaves for the southern mainland colonies, depended on trade with the French and Dutch islands. Only through this trade could his citizens pay for British manufactured goods. He then accused the Caribbean sugar planters of tyrannizing their fellow British colonists. Accustomed to "an arbitrary and cruel government over slaves, and hav[ing] so long tasted the *sweets* of oppressing their fellow creatures, they can hardly forbear esteeming two millions of free and loyal British subjects, inhabitants of the northern colonies, in the same light." Slavery was no metaphor: it was a struggle for life, the liberty of self-government, and property, for people of any race. As Hopkins put it in a treatise published later that year, Britain's "glorious constitution" guaranteed especially that no one ever be deprived of his property without his consent. "On the contrary, those who are governed by the will of another, or of others, and whose property may be taken from them by taxes, or otherwise, without their own consent, and against their will, are in the miserable condition of slaves."[6]

In a stroke the New Englanders had found a voice that seemed to solve their image problem. They might be slave traders, but they weren't slave masters, or slaves. They were better than the West Indians (and by implication the Virginians and South Carolinians, who had not as yet weighed in on the new taxes). The British constitution said so.

But where did it say so? And did it really apply to everyone? The openness of Britain's unwritten constitution created problems as well as opportunities for the colonists. James Otis stepped into this breach in response to the Sugar Act and pushed the antislavery logic even further. In *The Rights of the British Colonies Asserted and Proved* (1764), Otis turned his argument against political enslavement into a ringing attack on racial justifications for African enslavement, again associating such arguments with the West Indians. He backed off a bit by asserting that the northern colonies were in fact not "a compound mongrel mixture of *English, Indian* and *Negro*," but rather "freeborn *British white* subjects." If racial distinctions were to be made in determining constitutional rights, northern white colonists would remain insiders.[7] Nevertheless, Otis signaled an emerging tendency for the debate over British rights to spur a controversy over whether any slavery—political or racial—could be constitutional at all.

The metaphor of slavery was far too entrenched in British politics to be separated out from the colonial controversy, because it was more than a metaphor. The comparison of political liberties to bondage did not have to be discovered: it had been there from the start. If British freedom could be construed to mean that taxation without representation equaled enslavement, something had to give. Either colonists had to be defined as constitutionally unequal Britons, or taxes like the Stamp Act could be declared unconstitutional.

The heavy hitters in British politics saw the implications at once, and jumped into the debate as quickly as did leaders in the colonies. By 1765 a sizable contingent in Parliament wanted to resolve the question of the colonists' British identity and make it clear that colonists were *subjects*, rather than citizens, of the British Empire. Lord Mansfield, the chief justice of the Court of King's Bench and a member of the House of Lords, made the case most clearly. Not only were colonists just as subject to the laws of Parliament as everyone in England; they also "are more emphatically subjects of Great Britain than those within the realm." The sovereignty of Parliament over the entire empire remained indivisible, "whether such subjects have a right to vote or not."

By contrast, William Pitt, the former prime minister, said that this view amounted to the subjection of the colonists. "When were they made slaves?" he asked. He even suggested that if they had not protested the Stamp Act, they would have been acting like slaves, and the precedent of their slavishness would eventually help make slaves of Englishmen at home. With those alternatives on the table, voiced by leaders admired on both sides of the Atlantic, it is not surprising that Parliament repealed the taxes but passed a clause, later known as the Declaratory Act, stating that Parliament could legislate for the colonies "in all cases whatsoever."[8]

A pattern had been established that would persist for the

next decade. In a series of confrontations leading up to the imperial breach of 1776, colonists insisted on their constitutional equality, usually adding, as Otis later did, that they only objected to certain kinds of taxes. "Internal taxes" on purchased items were unacceptable, testified Franklin, but Americans had no objection to import duties paid at dockside. Import duties were unacceptable, wrote John Dickinson in his *Letters from a Farmer* (1767), if they sought to raise money rather than regulate trade, for to take people's money without their consent could end in the taking of any and all property, which was slavery. In each case, a minority in Parliament would support the colonial protesters, leading lobbyists like Franklin to hope for a changing of the guard and a new policy. In the end, the new or old administration would seek a practical compromise but insist upon the principle of colonial subjection. Franklin kept making proposals—such as an American parliament (Scotland had one), or a clear and permanent division of lawmaking powers—but they were destined to fail without real, decisive, and quick constitutional change within the empire.

And Franklin knew why. In his anonymous essays in the British press, he argued against the increasing tendency of the British to call the Americans "our colonists" or "our subjects." He insisted that only the king had subjects—which was everyone in the empire. It was impossible for the colonists to be the subjects of subjects. That's what slaves were legally: the subjects of subjects. If the white colonists were to be simply governed, or forced to behave, they were being treated like slaves! William Knox, the undersecretary of state for the American colonies, actually quoted Franklin as having told him that Parliament's right to tax Pennsylvanians "is equivalent to an authority to declare all white persons in that province Negroes." Knox himself responded elsewhere, perhaps sarcastically, that maybe it was time to recognize that African slaves, as subjects of the empire, had some British rights, if that's what it took to get the Americans to recognize that colonies were under the sovereign power of the empire. An anonymous English pamphlet writer focused on the language of slavery as used by the colonists, arguing that their very words signified rebellion. Turning around the colonists' accusations of a conspiracy against British liberties, he detected "a general conspiracy" of the colonies. "It is said, that taxing the colonies makes them, *ipso facto*, slaves. What a profanation of language! Has not every nation a right to colonize?"[9]

The debate had already become circular. To get out of it, American protesters focused on some strategies that worked better among themselves than in England. They began to theorize the nature of their rights: the extent to which they were grounded in the British constitution and their British birthrights or in nature itself. They also developed powerful strategies of popular mobilization that went beyond the largely urban crowd actions that had been organized against the Stamp Act. Most important of these was the boycott, or the nonconsumption and later nonimportation of certain goods.

The boycotts waxed and waned over a decade; they were especially tough on the merchants who first proposed them. But they had a remarkable democratizing potential. Anyone could say, *I will not consume British goods*; in fact it might be easier for poor than for rich people to say they wouldn't use the things that the British taxed, like paper or paint or tea. And anyone could help shame others who refused to go along. Their vigilance against threats to their liberties proved them to be anything but slaves. John Dickinson gave this sentiment its most popular expression in his "Liberty Song" of 1768:

> Come join hand in hand, brave Americans all,
> And rouse your bold hearts at fair Liberty's call;
> No tyrannous acts, shall suppress your just claim,
> Or stain with dishonor America's name.
> In freedom we're born, and in freedom we'll live;
> Our purses are ready,
> Steady, Friends, steady,
> Not as *slaves*, but as *freemen* our money we'll give.[10]

Patriotic nonconsumption—the refusal to buy certain objects and pay taxes on them—reduced the regional and class differences among white colonists. It inspired the participation of greater numbers of men and women. It was a wonderfully adaptive strategy, allowing people to unify around a common enemy even if they disagreed about the possible implications of resistance for the institution of slavery. Virginians like Thomas Jefferson joined in and promised to stop importing slaves as well, reducing the seeming contradiction of slaveholders demanding liberty to a seeming consistency (at least in their own eyes). Jefferson had proposed legislation aimed at reducing slavery in

Virginia before. In the 1774 pamphlet that made his reputation and earned him a seat in the first Continental Congress, Jefferson depicted the slave trade as something that the English government, with its restrictive trade rules, had foisted upon the colonists.[11]

Jefferson was unusual in his direct condemnation of slavery. Yet his desire to link slavery and the oppression of the colonies, and begin the end of both at one fell swoop, emerged under two integrally related political pressures. Together, these pressures loomed larger than the hypocrisy evident when slaveholders talked about the horrors of slavery.

The first pressure point resided in the slaves themselves, who found in the colonial controversy distinct opportunities to fight for their own liberties. There was nothing new about slaves rebelling, running away, petitioning for their liberty in individual cases, or suggesting that slavery was an abomination before God. In recent decades they had taken advantage of colonial wars and religious revivals to do all these things. Historians have detected heightened patterns of slave resistance—more fugitives, more rumors of rebellions and executions—occurring when open conflict flared within white society over colonial policy: in 1765, escalating in 1774 and 1775. By 1772 slaves had also begun to criticize slavery publicly with explicit references to natural rights and to the struggle of their white owners to achieve recognition of their British constitutional liberties.

The second pressure point developed when some whites amplified and encouraged claims for black constitutional liberties. The modern constitutional politics of slavery began in 1772 when black resistance, white British criticisms of slavery, and the imperial crisis converged in a profoundly important court case. Never again could British slaveholders reassure themselves that everybody (who mattered) believed in slavery as a traditional form of property. Their politics changed accordingly.

The decisive moment began when James Somerset, slave of a colonial customs official in Virginia, took the opportunity of a London voyage to run away. His master, Charles Steuart, tried to have him seized and made it clear that he intended to take him to the West Indies to be sold. Somerset sought the legal aid of Granville Sharp, a reformer who had criticized the hypocrisy of American slaveholders in an influential pamphlet. Sharp saw colonial slavery as an unconstitutional innovation, one that had the potential to corrupt England itself. Somerset's case struck him as an opportunity to save an individual from brutal violence and actually challenge the legality of slavery in England— or at least the recapture of fugitives in the home country.

James Somerset appeared before the chief justice of the Court of King's Bench, Lord Mansfield himself—the age's most important interpreter of the British constitution and, as we have seen, a major player in the debates about the colonies. And Mansfield decided the case narrowly in favor of Somerset's personal rights under the British constitution. He could not be kidnapped and sent abroad in the absence of a positive, parliamentary law of slavery.

The Mansfield decision immediately set off a wave of speculation about the end of slavery in England, fanned by the black community there, who sought to make facts on the ground, and to a significant extent succeeded in doing so. The arguable significance of this event in the history of slavery, however, has obscured its deeper logic, roots, and political implications. Mansfield pushed the envelope on fugitive slaves not because he hated the institution of slavery or thought its legality unproven but rather because it was a matter of parliamentary sovereignty over the local laws and practices of the colonies. He did exactly as he had done in the Stamp Act repeal debates seven years before. He declared the Americans subject to parliamentary statutes regardless of their local laws.

It is revealing that this crucial moment of truth in British Atlantic politics could emerge out of a court case involving a Virginia fugitive. Until recently, the case has not been considered politically significant in the colonial controversy, because it left no statutory trail. No public meetings denounced Lord Mansfield; his effigy did not hang in Charleston or Boston. Yet the Mansfield decision in the *Somerset* case demonstrated that slaveholders had at least as much to fear from parliamentary sovereignty as did merchants. It also suggested a problem with the judicial discretion exercised by the lord chief justice. Soon American lawyers like Jefferson would be denouncing Mansfield for what we would call judicial activism. They de-emphasized common-law traditions as interpreted by judges in favor of precisely written constitutions.

J.G.A. Pocock writes of a "Machiavellian moment" in the history of republics when political actors realize that republican political institutions, which depend on the virtue of citizens, are evanescent and corruptible, making both drastic action and the republic's fall inevitable.[12] On the imperial, Anglo-American side of this tradition we might also see a *Mansfieldian moment*, when it becomes impossible to deal with key constitutional questions without engaging in the politics of slavery. The slavery issue, in turn, became a fulcrum of constitutional change.

A rather conservative jurist who had no desire to threaten property, Mansfield agonized over the decision in *Somerset v. Steuart* and did his best to keep it limited to the case: it was for him, too, a Mansfieldian moment. The decision for Somerset then created another such moment for slaveholders, who had to either accept the decision or risk taking other actions that might prove just as disruptive to their rule. British constitutionalism à la Mansfield was a threat to slaveholders' property. Mansfield urged the members of Parliament to take up the matter of slavery's legalities. They might institute an empire-wide slave code. They might leave it up to local law in all matters that did not touch English soil. But it was up to Parliament. To Mansfield the lawyer, the beauty, the justice, the security, and the Englishness of it all lay in the details and the process of making constitutional distinctions. (This is why Mansfield remains a hero to constitutional lawyers.) To Americans like Jefferson and Franklin, the horror of it lay in the powers it removed from them as colonists.

Granville Sharp thought that Mansfield had not gone far enough—he should have declared slavery itself un-British and unconstitutional throughout the empire. In consultation with

Franklin and American abolitionists like Anthony Benezet, who were encouraged by the signs of antislavery sentiment as far south as Virginia, Sharp agreed to mute his criticisms of the colonists in favor of warnings against *British* hypocrisy in freeing some slaves while leaving the status of those across the water unaddressed. During 1773 and 1774, Franklin, by now the point man for all the colonies in London, similarly and vigorously blamed slavery's growth on British refusals to let the Americans regulate their own trade—the same argument the Virginians had been making in petitioning the Crown to let them restrict slave importation.

This, in any case, was the argument made publicly by leading colonists. In private, their consciences, and their confidence, had been shaken. The modern politics of slavery emerged in this distinction between beliefs stated in private and positions staked out in courts, in legislatures, and in printed public debates. Patrick Henry, Virginia's rising radical, admitted in a private letter to the antislavery activist Robert Pleasants that he agreed with Benezet and admired the Quakers "for their noble effort to abolish slavery. It is equally calculated to promote moral and political good."[13] In public, however, such an admission undermined the patriot cause. Jefferson and Franklin argued in print that the refusal to let the colonies free themselves from slavery was yet another proof of the administration's tendency to enslave the colonists.

Such statements provoked even more angry responses by critics, and contributed to the bitter personal dimension of the imperial crisis. Franklin found himself caught distributing private letters of the former lieutenant governor of Massachusetts for political effect even as he pleaded his loyalty to the Crown and Parliament. The Board of Trade responded by calling him on the carpet in a theater-like room known as the Cockpit. There they let Alexander Wedderburn, the highly skilled solicitor general, lambaste the colonial agent and postmaster general for two hours, culminating in comparisons to a letter-stealing thief and, finally, to a double-crossing "bloody African" slave character from a popular contemporary play. Pamphleteers made even more fun of the colonists' tendency to talk about their own enslavement. Responding to Franklin's "general practice to talk of 'slavery,' " Dr. Samuel Johnson suggested that perhaps the real slaves should be called out as soldiers to silence rebellious claims to colonial sovereignty. Improving upon William Knox's proposal for recognizing black subjects' rights, Johnson even suggested making African slaves the new colonial overlords: "They may be more grateful and honest than their masters."[14]

Subjection of the Americans and antislavery could go hand in hand. And if they did, replied Johnson's critics, it meant that Britain really intended to treat patriotic resisters as rebels, and rebels as slaves. In his famous speech before Parliament on conciliation with the colonies, delivered March 22, 1775, Edmund Burke spelled out the spiraling nature of the politics of slavery. The spiral would end in disaster, war, and possibly independence, Burke argued, because the Americans really were culturally Englishmen: their political experience had led them (in "error") to expect to run their own affairs. Recently they had all become "lawyers," reading the commentaries of Blackstone more avidly than the English themselves. The northern colonies were full of dissenting Protestants. In the South, where the Church of England remained strong, though, the presence of slaves made the whites even more "proud and jealous of their freedom. Freedom is to them not only an enjoyment, but a kind of rank and privilege . . . In such a people, the haughtiness of domination combines with the spirit of freedom, fortifies it, and renders it invincible."[15]

This rhetorical escalation became quite real. In July, Benjamin Franklin wrote to one of his British friends that the royal governors of North Carolina and Virginia had been "exciting an insurrection among the Blacks." Lord Dunmore, Virginia's governor, began to get information and assistance from local slaves, then threatened to arm slaves in defense of Crown government. When patriots took over armories and forced him offshore, Dunmore issued a proclamation on November 7 promising freedom to fugitive slaves who fought under his banner. Once again, as in the Mansfield case, African Americans helped turn rumors and possibilities into facts, telling each other that the whole purpose, or at least the likely result, of the expected British invasion of the South would be to liberate them. A similar set of events took place in South Carolina, where the idea that "they will all be sett free" became "common talk throughout the Province" among slaves. Military developments favored the patriots in both cases: the hastily assembled Crown forces did not retake Williamsburg or Charleston in 1775. But southern leaders looked fearfully toward the warmer fighting months of

1776. William Hooper, a delegate to the Congress from North Carolina, thought it a certainty that "our negroes are to be armed against us." The black-British alliance decisively pushed planters in these states toward independence.[16]

With slavery propelling wealthy planters toward revolution, it became harder to blame the British for slavery, or to preserve the across-the-board condemnation of slavery that made American protests seem consistent. Burke, revealingly, had not even tried. He simply noted that while it might be possible to subdue an American rebellion by promising freedom to slaves, what would prevent the Americans from arming their slaves as well? The hypocrisy argument could still be turned around against the empire, especially since the Americans had seized the moral high ground and stopped importing slaves. Burke did not find it necessary to take a stand on slavery in order to perceive how complicated, and crucial, the issue had become, not least because the actions of slaves themselves had to be understood as part of the political situation:

Slaves as these unfortunate black people are, and dull as all men are from slavery, must they not a little suspect the offer of freedom from that very nation which has sold them to their present masters?—from that nation, one of whose causes of quarrel with those masters is their refusal to deal any more in that inhuman traffic? An offer of freedom from England would come rather oddly, shipped to them in an African vessel, which is refused an entry into the ports of Virginia or Carolina, with a cargo of three hundred Angola negroes. It would be curious to see the Guinea captain attempting at the same instant to publish his proclamation of liberty, and to advertise the sale of his slaves.[17]

Fifteen months later, drafting the Declaration of Independence, Thomas Jefferson struggled with the same need to spin the spiraling politics of slavery. Could British guilt and American innocence be confirmed without advancing the cause of abolition? Did Jefferson even want to? The draft Declaration includes a telling paragraph denouncing the barbarism of the slave trade. The "Christian" king had lowered himself to the level of pirates and "*Infidel* powers" at the expense of innocent Africans and the colonists rendered powerless to end the trade. To add insult to injury, in Jefferson's version of history, the Crown had decided to wage war on the colonists using these same Africans, "thus paying off former crimes committed against the *liberties* of one people, with crimes which he urges them to commit against the *lives* of another." This passage was debated and cut out by the Continental Congress as a whole, but carefully preserved by Jefferson himself in his papers and included in his unfinished autobiography. Writing in 1821, in the wake of the controversies over slavery in Missouri, Jefferson blamed the South Carolinians, Georgians, and New Englanders for their "tender consciences" about slavery. Had it been up to him, the nation would have had an unambiguously antislavery statement in the Declaration, one that blamed the British yet criticized slavery too directly as far as people from the Deep

South and (if Jefferson's memory is to be trusted) some New Englanders were concerned.

Or perhaps the draft and revision functioned as a kind of therapy, an insurance policy against Jefferson's own bad conscience, or worse outcomes. It was not at all clear that the nation or slavery would survive a civil war. The revision process that eliminated the slavery passage and produced the final document suggests a growing concern with the fact of slaves in arms, as well as the compromises with slaveholding and slave-trading interests Jefferson remembered. Benjamin Franklin, who served on the drafting committee, suggested the insertion of "[He has] excited domestic insurrections among us" into the now-culminating accusation that the king had "endeavored to bring on the inhabitants of our frontiers the merciless Indian savages, whose known rule of warfare is an undistinguished destruction of all ages, sexes and conditions."[18] The revised Declaration, in other words, made slave insurrection, with Indian warfare, the latest and perhaps greatest example of the king's tyranny. The Declaration, then, had turned from antislavery in draft to anti-antislavery (if not proslavery) in publication.

It made sense politically to de-emphasize actual slaves in favor of the king's tyranny, and not to raise the question of America's future policy on slavery. Nevertheless, Jefferson the revolutionary, defeated in committee, could, along with John Adams, feel as if he had tried his best to seize the Revolutionary moment to give American slavery a fatal wound. The Declaration did not become the antislavery statement to "a candid world" that Jefferson may have hoped would help the new nation get foreign aid. Instead, proslavery steps had been taken, while antislavery feelings had been preserved.

British hopes to stab American independence in its soft southern underbelly stalled in 1775 and 1776. Wanting a quick military victory and not a civil war, the early British commanders attacked and captured the northern cities that had been the hotbeds of Revolutionary sentiment: Boston, New York, Philadelphia. They had more difficulty pacifying the extensive countryside, or bringing the continuing war for the frontiers to bear on the coastal struggle. As the war lengthened and spread to new areas in the North, more and more slaves found opportunities to use the conflict to run away or negotiate their freedom. Early on, New England militia and Continental army recruiters recognized this reality and enlisted free African Americans. General George Washington first discouraged the practice, then accepted it as inevitable given troop shortages.

In 1778, the stalemated British decided on a southern strategy, in part because they still believed that concern about property in slaves had kept significant numbers of white Southerners loyal to the Crown. All of the British Caribbean colonies had remained loyal. With the French now in the conflict, the English also wanted to guard their interests in the West Indies against French raids. British forces invaded Georgia and South Carolina. Slaves near the coasts provided key guidance in the fall of Savannah.

The actions of slaves, however, made the American war as unwinnable in the long run for the British as it had seemed promising in the short run. The American Revolution became a civil war in the South in part because of the ways that British forces tried to liberate the slaves of rebels while protecting the property of loyalists. This encouraged people in the Deep South, white and black, to do what people do during civil wars: take matters into their own hands. Slaves ran to British armies, Tories and rebels liberated (or stole) each other's slaves, and the slavery issue contributed to the escalation of the conflict. In 1780 and 1781, fugitive slaves helped make Lord Cornwallis's invading army a scourge as it marched through North Carolina into Virginia. But the sheer size of his army and its long train of followers made it difficult to sustain in the countryside, especially during an epidemic of smallpox. When higher British officials preferred to aid regiments in the West Indies and the North, Cornwallis found himself bound up with his thousands of African American allies near Yorktown—vulnerable to the attack by land and sea that cost him his army, and the British the war.[19]

The revolution to preserve British traditions had changed things, and it had liberated tens of thousands of slaves (recent estimates vary from 25,000 to 100,000). But it had also preserved slavery. The war had in part derived from the desire of slaveholders to protect their lives, their fortunes, and their sacred honor, goals they pursued by trying to keep hold of their slaves. The war had also seemed to continue the prewar trend in the North toward emancipation. Vermont eliminated slavery in its 1777 constitution; Massachusetts confirmed emancipation judicially during the 1780s; and Pennsylvania enacted a gradual emancipation scheme in 1780. On the other hand, the cash-strapped, invaded southern states had responded to the economics of civil war by promising white enlistees payment in (future) lands *and* slaves.

The new state constitutions, like the resistance movement and the Revolutionary War, moved in both directions with regard to slavery. In the short run, the very autonomy of the new states allowed them to avoid resolving this vexing issue collectively. The sheer variety, number, and geographical spread of the states, the very factor that had made it so hard for the British to conquer them, allowed the contradictory trends to continue. American liberty won the war; it undermined slavery in many places and in some minds, while in the end it confirmed slavery nationally.

Similar trends can be seen in the Continental Congress. One would not expect the notably, intentionally weak federal government to take up a controversial issue like slavery. On the other hand, wars have a tendency to expand government's scope by forcing executives and legislators to address issues that, as politicians, they would just as soon avoid. Recruitment policy formed an early, and repeated, example. Members of the Congress quickly became aware of each other's sensitivities to the question. In 1777, not long after what Thomas Paine described as "the times that try men's souls," John Adams agreed that the war effort required at least a temporary silence on slavery, and helped squash a bill enacting emancipation in Massachusetts. In 1776, the Virginian general George Washington, in constant dialogue with the supreme authority that had commissioned him, had accepted free black soldiers, thus helping to make the

American army more integrated than any American military force until the Vietnam War, at least during the war's northern phase. Yet Washington also consistently supported the policy—a fiction—that slaves did not serve in the American army. When the war moved south, though, southern delegates found themselves listening hard to their northern colleagues. The British had no official policy regarding the status of North American slaves as allies or combatants. Neither did the patriots. The Congress, including key South Carolina delegates, recommended arming several thousand slaves; the legislature of South Carolina turned it down in a huff. Still, some Northerners hoped that slave regiments would in the end be employed: "It will produce the Emancipation of a number of those wretches and lay a foundation for the Abolition of Slavery in America."[20]

The Congress's other immediate challenges forced it to deal with slavery. First, the Congress drew up and debated the Articles of Confederation, setting the rules and parameters of its own actions. This immediately required the Congress to deal with the problem of taxation—how it would raise money. The ensuing debates of July 30 to August 1, 1776, quickly grew heated and set key precedents for the battles at the Constitutional Convention in 1787.[21]

John Dickinson's draft form of government proposed that the states contribute to the national fund according to population, excluding only "Indians not paying Taxes." Samuel Chase of Maryland objected to counting slaves as people for the purpose of taxation because "Negroes [are] a Species of Property—Personal Estate." States with more slaves would in effect be paying according to both population and property, he argued, comparing slaves to cattle held by northern farmers. John Adams replied that counting people to determine taxes was not counting subjects or citizens. It was really only a convenient way of counting wealth, and slaves produced wealth as much as other people. The "laboring poor," after all, "are sometimes called slaves . . . to the state." The difference was "imaginary only."[22]

Adams was trying to articulate a theory of government that, with respect to taxation, could be silent about slavery. He had spent the past two years working with southern delegates to try to push them toward independence. A radical on the independence question, he was a social conservative who distrusted quick emancipation, and in the Congress he had tried to finesse the black soldier issue, much as his more radical cousin Samuel Adams had downplayed the links others made between the patriot and the antislavery causes in Massachusetts.[23] Silence about slavery would emphasize what the Americans had in common, such as a desire for equitable taxation grounded in the consent of the people.

But slaveholder interests would not allow for silence. Benjamin Harrison of Virginia tried to step in with a rational compromise: count two slaves for every freeman. It could be rationalized on grounds that might actually flatter Northerners: "He affirmed that slaves did not do so much work as freemen, and doubted if two effected more than one."[24]

The cat was out of the bag. Suddenly the Congress found itself debating not the means or ends of taxation but the nature

of slavery, exactly as Franklin had in trying to limn colonial taxation and political economy a quarter century before. James Wilson of Pennsylvania jumped in with enthusiasm. If slaves did
not count, southern states would have the wealth without being
taxed accordingly. Slaves did not produce less taxable wealth;
they produced more. They consumed, or received, less than
freemen, and both men and women worked the fields. Slaves
had to be guarded and did not usually serve as soldiers; they
"increase the burthen of defence," which would then mean
Northerners being taxed to defend white Southerners from
slaves. Because the Continental Congress had issued resolutions
against slave importation, Wilson could argue that "it is our
duty to lay every discouragement on the importation of slaves."
Chase's scheme of making slaves tax-free would actually give a
political incentive to importers of slave labor. Besides, Wilson
repeated several times, for every slave there is one less freeman
in America.

Morality aside, slavery itself was bad policy. Brought into
taxation, it would create inequality and perpetuate itself. Resi-
dents of the Deep South, however, seemed to want slaves discussed *only* as property, not as people rebelling or contributing to
the commonwealth. Thomas Lynch of South Carolina issued
the ultimatum: "If it is debated whether the slaves are their property, there is an end of the confederation . . . Freemen cannot be
got to work in our Colonies; it is not in the ability or inclination
of freemen to do the work that the negroes do." No slaves, no
South Carolina. Let's get back, Lynch insisted, to talking about
whether livestock should be taxed, too.

Nothing Wilson had said intimated that slaves might not belong to their owners. Nor had he raised the moral issue of hypocrisy. He had done worse: he had admitted the specter of Lord Mansfield. A stronger union, an American empire, might decide that slavery ought to be discouraged or regulated, despite the reality of property rights in slaves. Franklin, who spoke next or shortly afterward, may have actually lowered the heat by redirecting attention to Wilson's argument that "sheep will never make any insurrections." Such statements pointed to a real problem with slavery—slaves were people, and had a tendency to rebel—but everyone had been whispering about that for a year already, as Franklin had acknowledged with his emendation to the Declaration about the king having "excited domestic insurrections amongst us." It would be better, said Edward Rutledge of South Carolina, to simply "get rid of the idea of slavery" altogether. "The slaves do not signify property; the old and young cannot work." Silence was to be preferred to this return of the Mansfieldian moment.[25]

No one, including Rutledge, tried to justify slavery beyond asserting its necessity and Northerners' complicity. South Carolinians had threatened to walk before, when the Continental Congress at first refused to exempt their staple products, rice and indigo, from its non-exportation resolves of 1774. The debate demonstrated, though, that taxation raised thorny sectional as well as constitutional issues. Only a month after the debate over Jefferson's draft Declaration, slavery and its fruits had again emerged as a potential division among the new states.

The states north and east of Delaware joined to vote down Chase's motion. But the complications of the debates about taxation slowed the deliberations over the new form of government, helping to postpone its adoption and weaken its ultimate form. In October 1777, when it continued to revise the Articles, the Congress switched to land as a basis of taxation—an extremely impractical way of apportioning taxes on a national level because of fluctuating wartime land prices and the nonexistence of an administrative apparatus to survey and estimate land values. In March 1783, after a somewhat successful experiment with a tax on imports, the Congress switched back to population as a basis for taxes—but this time with a version of Harrison's compromise. Three-fifths of slaves would be counted for calculating each state's tax bill. James Madison proposed the ratio in order to prove his "liberality," Edward Rutledge seconded, and James Wilson agreed.[26]

Other compromises of 1777 introduced safeguards for slavery. In this draft, only "free inhabitants" were guaranteed protection of the law and the right to move themselves and their property from state to state. These distinctions, which had not been present in Dickinson's 1776 draft, repudiated Mansfield's ruling, which had established Somerset's British right of mobility over local laws enslaving him. The 1776 draft had also established the supremacy of the Congress in the United States in cases of a conflict of laws. The 1777 draft ratified by the states reversed this direct threat to the local law of slavery in its second article: "Each state retains its sovereignty, freedom, and independence, and every Power, Jurisdiction and right, which is not by this confederation expressly delegated to the United States."[27]

That local autonomy allowed all of the states to legislate

against the slave trade and some of the northern states to legislate against slavery itself. But local autonomy, written into the Articles, protected slavery on the national level even as the war, in the South and in small places all over the country, became the largest slave rebellion in American history. A creature of empire as much as of everyday life, slavery had already shown a striking tendency to haunt American politics, even as its leaders tried to free themselves from its grasp.

In this sense, the Revolution set, and the war confirmed, a colonial pattern. The revolutionaries created a politics of slavery that sought to dissolve or normalize the institution in euphemisms like "this species of property," only to find that slaves had a tendency to insist that they, too, were people who hated slavery. The Americans had emancipated themselves, but in doing so had raised, not resolved, the question of slavery. On both sides of the Atlantic, people waited to see what exactly Americans meant when they said they would never be slaves.

TWO

The Great Compromises of
the Constitutional Convention

American leaders gave ambiguous answers to the question of where they stood on slavery. The Declaration of Independence, as published, stated that all men are created equal, but the Congress sidestepped the issue of Africans as soldiers, treating them only as domestic insurrectionists. After British governors and generals issued proclamations freeing slaves who fought on their side, the patriots used those documents as anti-British propaganda. Slavery might be wrong, but slaves themselves were something worse: an enemy within.

The leading colonial agent in England, Benjamin Franklin, blamed slavery on the British and described British overtures to slaves as the final proof of their tyranny. Once independence had been declared, though, Franklin sailed for France and found more to be gained there by emphasizing an American antislavery future. This future might only exist if the new states gained French diplomatic recognition and aid. In a reply to inquiries by would-be immigrants titled *Information to Those Who Would Remove to America* (1784), Franklin insisted that newcomers to the states must not expect to have slaves to work for them: in the United States, people worked for themselves. To prove the point, Franklin told a story in which a slave with a West Indian accent describes his amazement at how hard white men tended to work. The notion of the United States as the opposite of slavery and of other European forms of oppression was so important to Franklin and the patriots during the early 1780s that Franklin, the most careful of writers, left unanswered the question of what the slave in the story was doing and whom he was doing it for when he wasn't offering testimony on the work habits of the master class.[1]

Franklin's successor as minister to France, Thomas Jefferson, also understood that the United States' international reputation could turn on how it spun the slavery question. Leading thinkers in France wanted to see the new republican nation as a cradle of liberty, even if only to use the comparison to promote reforms in France. When a French envoy asked the governors of the new American states to supply written answers to his questionnaire about their domestic governments and economies, Jefferson wrote and rewrote an answer aimed at a European audience. His *Notes on the State of Virginia*, first published in Paris (1785) and London (1787), defended the natural bounties and economic prospects of his "country" at great length. It also criticized slavery as the main flaw in the "manners" of the Virginians. The work is better known today for hypothesizing that African peoples might be naturally inferior, and for stating that the injuries of slavery meant that blacks and whites could never live side by side in freedom. Those highly charged and significant conclusions are put forward almost tentatively, as if to compensate for Jefferson's unambiguous indictment of slavery as bad for both blacks and whites. When the work is considered in its postwar moment, it is striking just how *defensive*, as well as ambiguous and contradictory, it seems on the race issues of the day. Jefferson desperately wanted his French and English sympathizers to believe that America had a future without slavery—not in the least because making them believe so would help ensure that America had a future at all.[2]

The early 1780s appear in retrospect as a high-water mark of Revolutionary radicalism with respect to the slavery question. Some contemporaries saw it as the beginning of the end. The trend toward gradual emancipation did not seem to be restricted to New England and Pennsylvania. The Virginian James Madison bought nine hundred acres of newly conquered land in New York's Mohawk valley as one of "several projects" he hoped would allow him to "depend as little as possible on the labour of slaves." When Billy, one of his slaves, ran away and was recaptured, Madison told his father that it would be wrong to sell him "merely for coveting that liberty for which" Americans had fought.[3]

If leaders of Virginia, the largest state, with more than 40 percent of its population enslaved, seemed to waver, who could know what the future held? Thomas Jefferson devised an emancipation plan for a revised Virginia constitution, he proudly told readers of his *Notes*, but his committee did not actually bring the plan before the legislature. While serving in the Congress in

1784, Jefferson proposed a ban of slaves in the western territories after 1800 that came within one vote of being adopted. That vote belonged to one of his Virginia colleagues.

Some Virginians freed their slaves, individually and sometimes as a group, especially after the state made it easier to do so in 1782. Others, alarmed at the threat these trends posed to their property, petitioned against the "partial Emancipation" they saw proceeding in the state. Asserting that "a Great number of slaves taken by The British army are now passing in this Country as Freemen," they urged greater policing of free African Americans. Other petitioners cited their contributions to the Revolutionary War to justify their defense of "the full, free, and absolute Enjoyment of every species of our Property." To these pro-slavery petitioners, antislavery legislation—even in the form of permission to free individuals—amounted to another attempt to take away men's "liberty and Property." Its advocates could only be "Enemies of our Country, Tools of the British Administration" who wanted to continue the war by other means.[4]

Even at the high point of Revolutionary antislavery, then, the trends went in several directions at once. Both emancipation measures and resistance to them can be seen as fruits of the new state governments formed by the revolutionaries. The republicanism of the new state constitutions, with weak executives and strong, often annually elected legislatures, elicited considerable discussion in Europe, and leading founders like John Adams wrote defenses of them. These legislatures had a new freedom to restrict, contain, or encourage slavery. In the northern states, the trend seemed clearly toward abolition. Vermont outlawed slavery in 1777, Pennsylvania freed the children of slaves gradually by a 1780 statute. Connecticut and New Hampshire followed suit in 1784. In New York and Virginia, the defeat of anti-slavery legislation could be read as a backlash or as just a temporary slowing of the inevitable trend toward emancipation. In the Carolinas and Georgia, though, few doubted that the slaves and British had lost the war—or that the victors saw slaves as the spoils. Given this inconsistency, little wonder then that descriptions of the new nation put forward by leading Americans sidestepped the slavery issue, associating the institution with the past, not the glorious future best exemplified by the more moderate, balanced new state constitutions.

According to middle-American (that is, upper-southern and lower-northern) aspirations, stated most explicitly and eloquently by Jefferson and Franklin, free government would lead to free society. America would lead the way. Yet the freedom to legislate their domestic institutions toward or away from human bondage was the same freedom that permitted the new states to ignore or sidestep the wartime requisitions of the Continental Congress. Renewed debates during 1781 and 1783 in the Congress over whether or how to count slaves for taxation would not have been necessary had the Articles of Confederation empowered the Congress to actually collect its taxes.

The Revolutionary War had been long and expensive. The Congress barely kept an army in the field. At key moments, such as after Washington's crossing of the Delaware, militia and civilians harassed the British army enough to make the patriots' retreat-and-attack strategy successful. Just as important, though, resistance to service far beyond home kept citizen armies small and vulnerable. In Virginia, the desire to hold on to slaves created a real disincentive for masters to serve, leaving the state vulnerable at both its coast and its frontier. When the British returned in 1780–81, more slaves fled to British lines. Only massive influxes of French aid, and French naval pressure on the British islands in the Caribbean, set the stage for the decisive Yorktown campaign.

Stubborn localism handicapped the Continental army but also helped exhaust the British, who repeatedly lost ground when they tried to turn battlefield victories into the pacification of the American countryside. Localism during wartime also translated into continental borrowing and rampant inflation. The new state legislatures, more responsive to constituents than ever before, limited the demands they would make on taxpayers and made local defense their priority instead of contributions to the continental government. Those economic pressures, in turn, put profound burdens on the states to pay the debts already incurred. In each state, people disagreed on whom and what to tax to pay the debt, and how to use other powers of the state to take in revenue—for example, through customs duties and paper-money schemes. The original issues of the American Revolution—how to pay for postwar debts and the process of making such decisions—had literally come home to the states. And failure to ratify the Articles of Confederation—in part because of those repeated arguments about whether to tax or represent slaves—made it more pressing and thus more difficult to make collective decisions about how to pay. Or even how to decide how to pay.

Much depended on the revival of trade. Optimists like Thomas Paine had predicted that America would feed the world. Unfortunately, the American dream of free trade did not appeal to the imperial powers that had spent so much on the American war. In the 1783 Orders in Council, England closed its West Indies colonies to the Americans. France and Spain watched as the states, bucking taxes, spoiled the Continental Congress's promises to pay off foreign loans. Some states even passed their own import and export taxes–in effect treating each other as foreign nations.

These conflicts set neighboring states against each other as rivals for frontier lands and seaborne trade. In the mid-1780s, however, trade issues also pointed to a widening geographical split between northern (sometimes called eastern) states and southern, slaveholding states. At the beginning, New Englanders worried most that their interests–such as their demands for fishing rights in the North Atlantic–would be sacrificed, with the help of New Yorkers, to the needs of Virginians and South Carolinians for the right to market their produce directly abroad. William Gordon, a member of the Continental Congress from Massachusetts, wrote in September 1782 that the United States had to "remain a collection of Republics, and not become an Empire . . . if America becomes an Empire, the seat of government will be to the southward, and the northern States will be insignificant provinces." Dealing with his colleagues from other states had increased his sense of regional differences. "Empire will suit the southern gentry; they are habituated to despotism by being the sovereigns of slaves; and it is only accident and interest that had made the body of them the temporary sons of liberty" during the war.[5]

These sorts of sectional explanations had been heard

before, but they had been muzzled during the earlier years of the war, when New Englanders and southerners had made common cause. Talking about slavery was becoming, once again, a way of addressing a range of political and economic issues. It could even define America, or Americans. When the French nobleman the Marquis de Chastellux wrote a book about his travels in North America, Jefferson, who was highly praised in the book, objected to Chastellux's depiction of Virginians as attached to their own interest. The marquis also described young Virginia planters "constantly talking about abolishing slavery"; Jefferson did not dispute that picture, but he didn't like the implication that slavery made Virginians more greedy or interested than other Americans, because this would mean that they were not likely to be the best citizens—or leaders.

Whatever the vices that slavery brought, attachment to interest was really a *northern* vice, Jefferson insisted, laying out the relative characteristics of Americans on a north-south axis:

IN THE NORTH THEY ARE	IN THE SOUTH THEY ARE
cool	fiery
sober	Voluptuary
laborious	indolent
persevering	unsteady
independant	independant
jealous of their own liberties, and just to those of others	zealous for their own liberties, but trampling on those of others
interested	generous

chicaning	candid
superstitious and hypocritical in	without attachment or pretensions to
their religion	any religion but that of the heart.

Pennsylvanians, wrote Jefferson, seemed to be "free from the extremes of vice and virtue," but New Yorkers, despite being farther north than Pennsylvania, were more southern. What could explain this anomaly? Jefferson did not need to mention that New York had tens of thousands more slaves than Pennsylvania and had not done anything to emancipate them.[6] Jefferson's ability to simultaneously criticize his slavery-based Virginia culture and yet compare it favorably with northern "interested" behavior is a typically eloquent expression of the postwar statesman's intertwined ambivalence about slavery and nationality. Local interests were sometimes regional, and had to be defended; yet local interests were also vices. The job of the statesman was to look above and beyond as well—something, Jefferson implied, New Englanders were unlikely to do, even though they displayed justice to Africans.

Jefferson may also have been thinking of what had occurred in the Continental Congress since his return from his first diplomatic tour in France. Latent regionalism became politically useful to explain and deal with voting patterns and shifting alliances in the Congress. The rules of the Congress, with one vote per state and nine votes out of thirteen necessary to pass any measure, made regional alliances as transparent as they were necessary. It probably didn't help that members of the Congress sat, and voted during roll call, by geography, beginning on one side of the room with New Hampshire and ending on the other side with Georgia.

In 1783 the Congress had decided to pass a tax to support the pay of the Continental army. Three years later, though, legislatures from both sides of the Mason-Dixon Line had still not ratified the requisite change to the Articles of Confederation because of concerns about how persons and property would be taxed. Slavery continued to prevent a long-term solution to the Confederation's problems of governance, and it played into the rising regionalism in the Congress.[7]

A number of nationalists in the Congress, mostly from Virginia and the larger mid-Atlantic states Pennsylvania and New York, argued that the power of the states and the weakness of the Confederation rendered the new nation, in effect, defenseless. The nationalists in the Congress held sway from 1781 to 1783, but afterward a number of them, including Madison, returned to their states because of the three-year term limits for delegates to the Congress.

Territorial issues, including the disposal of western lands won or secured during the war, set states in competition but also created the promise, or potential, of a federal future in which key issues would be resolved by consensus or compromise. Virginians claimed the most western land: Could they broker key territorial issues in the Congress? Jefferson saw the window of opportunity during his committee's work on the first of a series of land ordinances for the territories. He almost succeeded in winning a vote for a prohibition on slavery in all of the western territories after 1800–but other Southerners, including his fellow Virginia delegates, voted him down.

What is striking is not only that a Virginia vote (and, Jefferson insisted, the attendance of one more delegate from New Jersey) could have created a winning regional alliance against the Deep South but also that Jefferson believed that the Continental Congress had the power to limit the rights of slaveholders to take their property into the new territories. In 1785, James Monroe, a protégé of Jefferson and Madison, called for greater powers for the federal government over commerce—seemingly an "eastern" cause. Having given up their claims to expansive lands in the Ohio valley, some Virginians looked to the nation, not just the state, to secure an economic future that might not be mainly about plantations worked by slaves. Unable to convince Virginians to move decisively against slavery, Jefferson and his friends looked farther to the west, and to a federal government in which enlightened Virginians could, hopefully, pursue alliances for their own and for the greater good. In the short run, though, western and territorial issues fed the north-south divide, making it harder for would-be reformers in the Congress to regulate the economy on the national level.[8]

With both Britain and France taking advantage of American divisions, it seemed especially important to negotiate a treaty with Spain, whose territories bordered much of the American South. The Spanish, however, were more concerned with the Americans flooding into their border areas. Seeking to avoid competition and conflict with the rapidly multiplying Americans, Spain denied them the navigation of the Mississippi River. As John Jay negotiated with the Spanish minister Diego de Gardoqui, it became clear—to Jay at least—that the United States had little to negotiate with and that the best it could do was get the right to trade with Spain itself in exchange for accepting the ban of Americans from the Mississippi trade.

The problem was that Southerners—especially Virginians and North Carolinians—saw in expansion to the southwest and the port of New Orleans a solution to the problem of British and French intransigence about the terms of trade with their Caribbean colonies. A letter from Kentucky quoted in a Maryland newspaper went so far as to suggest that such a Spanish treaty would ruin all attempts to cultivate tobacco and as a result would "banish slavery," though the writer also worried that no other labor system could be profitable in those lands.[9] Only New England would benefit from the Spanish concession of the right to ship directly to Spain and its colonies. When New Yorkers and New Englanders in the Congress fudged the voting rules and allowed Jay to go against his explicit instructions not to give up navigation rights (the Congress was having trouble getting the quorum that would allow for the required nine of thirteen votes by state), the Mississippi question became a constitutional crisis as well. While some Westerners planned a breakaway state and a separate deal with the Spanish, Virginians began to realize the need to work closely with the middle states to protect their vision of the future.

By 1786, the Congress could hardly transact any business at all; not enough of its members bothered to attend. Madison sponsored a resolution in the Virginia legislature to call a national convention in Annapolis, Maryland, to solve the problem of rules of commerce among the states. But Madison's Annapolis Convention did not even receive a delegation from its host state. It took a sense of domestic crisis, in addition to the stalemate over foreign affairs, to drive enough leaders into the nationalist camp and make the next step—a convention to revise the Constitution—possible in 1787.

Anger at the political results of debt and taxes in the states inspired radical, even violent, protest at the local level between 1785 and 1787. In Massachusetts, armed farmers sought to put off foreclosures by preventing courts from doing their business. Officials called it a "rebellion" and sent out an army, only to lose the state elections to those who championed debtor relief. The popularity of Shays's Rebellion, even among some of those who scratched their heads at Revolutionary War veterans taking up arms against their own elected government, gave the otherwise regionally conscious New England officials a heightened awareness, in 1787, that they could not solve even their local political problems on their own. Similar events occurred in Pennsylvania, where the leaders most committed to elite control of the economy, and most worried about foreign investment, wanted to remake both the state and the national government "to insulate critical government powers," such as taxation and the money supply, "from popular control."[10] During these months, Madison, who was excitedly reading works of political theory and history sent over from France by Jefferson, wrote at least as compellingly about the threat to private property embodied by the pro-debtor-relief measures of the state legislatures as he did about the weakness of the Confederation in foreign affairs. As a result, the divisions and alliances that slavery made, which in 1784 seemed useful for fighting real political battles, receded into the background in 1787 as the state legislatures chose delegates to send to Philadelphia to discuss revisions to the Articles of Confederation.

Even as sectional consciousness waned in the state and national realm, another very different set of developments occurred among opponents of slavery. Emboldened in part by the negative publicity surrounding a United States that seemed neither to pay its debts nor to move against slavery, activists on both sides of the Atlantic devoted new energy, and savvy, to a public campaign to end the slave trade. They placed more and more antislavery writings in the British and American press. They recruited non-Quakers like Benjamin Franklin into new leadership roles in antislavery organizations such as the revitalized Pennsylvania Abolition Society. They emphasized the sponsorship of elites rather than the inspiring protests by people of African descent that had been so notable during the early 1770s. In Pennsylvania and New York, the antislavery societies began to work on petitions to be presented to the upcoming Constitutional Convention itself.[11]

Gradual emancipation had already been enacted in Pennsylvania seven years before, but these antislavery activists, like the nationalist founding fathers, saw a need, and an opportune moment, to think bigger. Franklin typified that realization. Having promised to "act in concert" with antislavery activists as many as fifteen years before, Franklin could hardly turn down a request to serve as head of an antislavery organization in his home state, particularly now that he had finished his term as president of Pennsylvania and had more or less announced his political retirement. When Franklin also agreed during the spring of 1787 to serve as one of Pennsylvania's delegates to the Constitutional Convention in Philadelphia, he became, in a sense, the embodiment of two trends—toward a larger, more prominent antislavery movement, and toward a stronger national government—at the same moment, in the same place, in the same person. The optimism that surrounded the abolition societies and the Constitutional Convention in 1787, both praised in the press in part because of their sponsorship by statesmen like Franklin, is easily forgotten because of subsequent events that turned them into institutions differing both in spirit and in kind.[12]

For a few months, the real politicking occurred in the Pennsylvania State House, after the Constitutional Convention delegates began to arrive in May, and in private conversations during the evenings. The Virginians converged first, more than a week before there were enough delegates to really begin the convention's work. They took the lead in proposing a new form of government rather than a revision of the Articles.

Before the Virginians made their proposal, the convention set several rules that had great consequences for the nature of its deliberations. The Irish-born planter Pierce Butler of South Carolina proposed a "news blackout." Not only would the delegates keep the windows shut during a Philadelphia summer; they promised not to leak any information about their deliberations. Just as important, a North Carolina delegate proposed that members of the convention be permitted to change their votes on reconsiderations of important questions. The Constitutional Convention created a relatively open venue for deliberation. Secrecy made possible the candor and brilliance of the debates so evident in James Madison's notes on the convention.[13]

These closed-door procedures went against an important trend of the Revolutionary era toward publicity and popular participation in politics. That is why Thomas Jefferson called the secreted convention an "abominable precedent." Modern commentators, apparently lacking Jefferson's enthusiasm for public opinion, tend to praise the founders for intentionally restricting democracy at just the right moment so that a foundation for democracy could be laid.[14] In any case, secrecy enabled the framers to speak with frankness, even to the point of "thinking out loud," about issues as touchy as the relationship of slavery to government; in this fashion, compromises could be explored. It made deliberations long, far longer than the delegates would have liked. On June 1 the veteran legislator George Mason predicted they'd be holed up until August—and he underestimated. The length of the meetings, in turn, made appeals to fundamental problems like slavery, and compromises on them, more attractive.

In a narrow sense, slavery was "not on the agenda" of the framers of the Constitution when they assembled.[15] Secrecy made it possible for it to emerge explicitly anyway, and surprisingly quickly. The two plans brought by members to the convention both alluded to the institution of slavery in their schemes of representation. The delegates noticed this instantly. Nothing was more important to the framers of the Constitution than representation. From the beginning of the convention, the great issues of representation and state sovereignty became entwined with the question of slaves as taxable wealth and as persons in, but seemingly not of, the polity. From there, the story of the Constitutional Convention became one of working not only around slavery but through it, to re-create republican government in a national union.

Edmund Randolph, the lean and thoughtful governor of Virginia and the acknowledged leader of his delegation, introduced the fourteen-point Virginia Plan on May 30 by describing the limits of the Articles of Confederation and the "absolute necessity of a more energetic government," both in foreign affairs and vis-à-vis the popular state governments, where "the powers of government exercised by the people swallows up the other branches." The convention sitting as a committee of the whole quickly agreed to design a government with three branches—legislative, executive, and judicial.[16]

Then the controversies began. Randolph proposed an ambiguous resolution fixing representation in the national legislature according to either "quotas of contribution" or "the number of free inhabitants." The larger point was to make the national government more representative of the population, not just the states—but Randolph had already managed to bring up the problem that had plagued the Continental Congress: Under proportional representation (or taxation), which inhabitants counted for what? The "quotas of contribution" most recently passed by Congress would include three-fifths of the slaves.

The acute and scholarly James Madison, a veteran of the Continental Congress between 1780 and 1783, had been through this before. Quick on his feet, he suggested that "free inhabitants"—language that could not but imply an answer to the slavery question—"would divert the Committee from the general question whether the principle of representation should be changed." The real question was whether or not to move away from the Continental Congress's one-vote-per-state procedure. But another young nationalist, the brilliant, walleyed Alexander Hamilton of New York, moved to keep "free inhabitants" in. The motion was then postponed.

Madison then tried another way, in his words, "to get around the difficulties." He and Randolph proposed that votes in the legislature be proportioned somehow, "and not according to the present system" of one vote per state. This call for an "equitable ratio" to be determined later was "generally relished," according to Madison—until Pennsylvania's Joseph Reed urged another postponement of the question. The delegates from Delaware had been forbidden by their instructions from their legislature to agree to any new scheme of voting in the Congress. Madison protested that for the new government to be truly national, it had to represent the people as a whole—not just the states. So ended the first day of the convention.[17]

In one day the delegates had traveled from representation to apportionment, around slavery, and back to the problem of national sovereignty. Could the convention keep slavery off the table long enough to resolve the principle of representation? It may have seemed so for a few days. The large-state, mid-Atlantic perspective that had Hamilton championing representation according to "free inhabitants" provoked a crucial debate about the future of the small states in a national government where they might not have much power. The more sophisticated small-state representatives like Roger Sherman of Connecticut and Elbridge Gerry of Massachusetts proceeded to invoke suspicions of democratic excess on behalf of the status quo of equal state representation in the national legislature.

This forced proponents of the Virginia Plan to spell out exactly what they intended: a supreme national government, the legitimacy of which would come directly from the people, but which would actually serve as a check on the excesses of democracy within the states themselves. Such an admission made the nationalists vulnerable to critiques by both democrats and localists. Consequently, it was Virginia's James Madison himself who was the first to bring the question of slavery explicitly into the debates. He did so somewhat defensively, on June 6, as part of a passionate speech about creating a truly republican, as well as supreme, national government, to secure justice and rights, especially rights to property. He used slavery, when justified by race, as an example of what was wrong with too much democracy: "We have seen the mere distinction of colour made in the most enlightened period of time, a ground of the most oppressive dominion ever exercised by man over man."[18]

Astute commentators have argued that whenever Madison brought up slavery in the convention, including on this occasion, he was really trying to distract the delegates from other conflicts, such as those between small states and big ones like

Virginia. But this misses the shape and nature of the process by which slavery repeatedly entered the conversation. It did so because slavery had already become entwined with the practical as well as theoretical debates about federalism, democracy, representation, and taxation. Madison wasn't being cynical: he was being intelligent, if ambitious. As David Brian Robertson has observed, Madison's remarks "validated the open discussion of slavery and other material interests, even though Madison's own strategy depended on establishing agreement on abstract principles before considering such substantive issues."[19] In the case of slavery as in other matters, our understanding of Madison the great strategist of federalism needs to be balanced by an appreciation of the Madison who was perhaps too theoretically astute to convince his more practically minded peers to think critically in these deliberations about the relationship between slavery for Africans and majority rule for whites. Madison brought up slavery not to distract the delegates but to get them to work through the intertwined issues of nationhood, sovereignty, representation, and property in people.

His gambit, in other words, did not convince immediately or easily because of its depth of insight and its abstract nature. Still, it helped shape the debate. Alexander Hamilton, for one, understood what was at stake: a vision of national government that might enable the kind of statesmanship it would take to end slavery. In some notes he took that same day, which he titled "Madison's Theory," Hamilton wrote that in an extended republic, "a process of election [could be] calculated to refine the representation of the People"—that is, to get around democracy's limitations. Hamilton was entranced by Madison's theory, but he also jotted down his opinion that sectional and other economic issues would reappear, regardless of the refinement process.[20] Madison did not disagree. He hoped that a larger sphere for representative government—the nation itself—would simultaneously limit, protect, and purify the pursuit of local interests.

A truly national government remained a hard sell to delegates who saw the democratic dimensions of state power; who simply wanted, or felt pledged, to protect their home institutions; or who did not identify with the enlarged "sphere" that Madison and Hamilton presumed they, as the talented tenth of the new nation, would naturally lead. And so the convention remained hung up on apportionment in the legislative branch for six long weeks.

This meant getting held up by slavery. Every time a major decision was made about the nature of representation, which the delegates rightly assumed would critically shape taxation, the slavery question came to the fore again, shifting the votes and muddying the waters. Elbridge Gerry of Massachusetts, in a June 11 speech Madison declined to record in his otherwise-copious notes, angrily asked why slave property should count as population, bringing back the old Yankee question of July 30, 1776: Why not count our cows then? According to the personally popular but acid-tongued Pierce Butler, however, Gerry went further, turning his reprise of old arguments into a stump speech: "Are we to enter into a Compact with Slaves. No! Are the Men of Massachusetts to put their hands in our purses. No!"[21]

This rhetorical displacement of the slave South's political

power onto the slaves themselves was meant to capture the irony, and the double wrong, of the three-fifths clause. Such voices are relatively absent in the record, though they would surface often in sectional politics after 1787. What is striking here is that the accusation is one of theft, accomplished through politics. It is not about race any more than it is about the inherent wrongs of slavery. The earlier compromises of 1776 and 1783 creating the federal ratio made it impossible for statesmen and framers like Gerry to think of slavery without thinking about property and power. This made it harder to deal with slavery, and impossible to avoid dealing with it either.

Gerry didn't get three-fifths taken out of the Virginia Plan, but he surely had something to do with Benjamin Franklin's first speech before the convention that day. Franklin had seen Gerry operate in France, and he preferred a more diplomatic style. The oldest delegate observed that the question of representation had caused the delegates to lose their "coolness & temper": he urged compromise by both large and small states. The delegates then confirmed proportional representation in the first branch of the legislature by a vote of 7 to 3 to 1 (Maryland split). Pierce Butler and John Rutledge of South Carolina immediately moved that the proportion be decided by the "quota of contribution" from 1783. James Wilson and Charles Pinckney moved to add the three-fifths clause explicitly, in the language of the Articles in 1783: "in proportion to the whole number of white and other free Citizens and inhabitants of every age sex and condition, including those bound to service for a term of years, and three fifths of all other persons not comprehended in the foregoing description, except Indians, not paying taxes in each State."

The center, or at least a nationalist–Deep South alliance, had seemed to hold—but only for the lower, now called "popular," house of the Congress. The delegates proceeded to split over whether to seat members of an upper house by the same proportional scheme of representation or by the Confederation rule of one vote per state. Gerry and Pinckney complicated things further with a motion that money bills had to originate in the popular branch.[22]

According to the tenacious, plainspoken, and always politic Roger Sherman of Connecticut, everything depended on whether the small states would get their way in the other house of the legislature. New Jersey's William Paterson asked for a day to prepare a counterproposal, a "primarily federal" structure of government later known as the New Jersey Plan. Paterson and Sherman's central goal was to preserve state sovereignty. In one of the New Jersey Plan's enduring yet unnoticed contributions to the Constitution, they proposed to recommit the new government to the three-fifths formula for taxation as well as representation.

Doing this served two ends. It reduced the political advantage of the both large and southern states in the lower house, by tying their increase in voting power to their tax burden. It also re-created the wedge that made Virginia's interests somewhat different from those of South Carolina and Georgia. In the process, the revised federal ratio, or three-fifths clause, began to erode the alliance between large states and southern states.

The use of the slavery issue to both defend and attack the

plan tells the story. Madison responded to Paterson's plan by stating that the kind of pure republican theory behind the defense of small-state prerogatives was in fact ridiculous given the politics of slavery. Under slavery, "the Republican Theory becomes still more fallacious," because no pure system of representing the majority of the people could be devised when so many of the people were slaves. In response, Luther Martin, a delegate from small slaveholding Maryland, invoked slavery to support state sovereignty. Slavery epitomized the diversity of the states, the reason why they could not legislate for one another.[23]

In part because of these contradictions, the New Jersey Plan could not itself gain enough adherents to turn the convention away from proportional representation as a means of compromise. On June 19, the convention rejected the New Jersey Plan and accepted the Virginia Plan. The ambiguity about representation in the second house remained unresolved, and delegates began to realize that their opinion on the matter might depend on what exactly that second house was going to be responsible for, and why.

By the third week of June, rumors had escaped the statehouse that the convention was getting nowhere fast, even though they had moved beyond initial committee-of-the-whole discussions and now sat "in convention" on the key issues of representation. One delegate told a member of the Congress that they wouldn't finish until October: "Very little is done and nothing definitive." On June 28, in the midst of a three-day speech by the loquacious, poorly dressed, and not well-liked Luther Martin on the states as guardians of liberties, Franklin offered a resolution for morning prayers led by a local clergyman. Hugh Williamson noted that the convention didn't have money to hire a regular preacher. Randolph suggested a special Fourth of July sermon, and the delegates could lead their own morning prayers. With frustrations mounting, finally, on the thirtieth, the delegates took up a resolution for equal votes in the Senate.[24]

What should the Senate be about? Small-state delegates said it should protect their sovereignty; others, following John Adams's recent treatise on republican government, insisted that an upper house should protect property from the vagaries of the more popular or democratic branch. Madison was sympathetic to this view, but he evidently feared an alliance between those skeptical of too much democracy, like himself, and the small states. Such an alliance could result in a constitution that would hamstring federal power.

Madison tried again to break the deadlock by arguing that the real conflict between the states was caused "not by their difference of size, but by other circumstances; the most material of which resulted partly from climate, but principally from the effects of their having or not having slaves. These two causes concurred in forming the great divisions of the U. States. It did not lie between large & small States: it lay between the Northern & Southern." Perhaps, instead of five freemen counting for three slaves, one branch could represent only the free, and the other all the people, slave and free. Unfortunately, though, admitted Madison, this would inevitably create some kind of inequality, because the branches could not and should not be exactly the same in their composition and duties.[25]

Much seems to depend on how we understand this second attempt by Madison to use slavery to resolve a crisis regarding representation. But we need not choose between the stark alternatives of viewing Madison's proposal, which was seconded by no one, as a disingenuous attempt to distract the delegates from their arguments about state power and antidemocratic impulses or as Madison's candid appraisal of slavery's centrality in American society and politics. It may be best to see it as both, because then we can appreciate Madison's growing boldness as a designer of a strong national government that could weld together all the conflicts, the risks, and the opportunities into a structure that would engineer balance. Indeed, he was making a point about the need for balance amid factors like slavery, an epitome of imbalance. He would pivot the Constitution on slavery, ignore slavery, or do both, as long as it preserved the "equilibrium of interests."

In this he had help. Franklin leaped in with a seemingly complicated revision: equal representation in the second branch where it concerned issues of state and federal power, but not where it concerned money questions. With Madison and Franklin making up compromises on the spot, and the convention running out of time before the July 4 holiday, the delegates voted one more time on equal state representation in the Senate. It came out a deadlock, 5 to 5. The only consensus that emerged was that a "Grand committee" needed to meet to address the representation question over the short vacation. Maryland's ever dramatic Luther Martin gave the committee members an extra incentive to get the job done by echoing the old threats of the

South Carolinians over slavery, but in a new, small-state key: "You must give each state an equal suffrage, or our business is at an end."[26]

The Grand Committee, made up of a delegate from each state, met at Franklin's house for dinner, where the host brought forward what has come to be known as the Connecticut Compromise. In the first branch of the legislature, there would be one representative for every forty thousand free inhabitants plus three-fifths of the slaves. All appropriations and taxes would come from that branch. In the second branch, the Senate, each state would have an equal vote.[27]

When the committee reported back to the convention, the proponents of the Virginia Plan did not hide their irritation. The committee exceeded its mandate, sputtered James Wilson. Madison did not see the provision for money bills to come out of the House as much of a concession by the smaller states. He had a point. The compromise that broke the deadlock and created the equal representation of states in the Senate lay rather in tying the democratic branch decisively to the "southern" interest. Not only would three-fifths of the slaves be represented there, but the extra power would inform all decisions regarding government spending and taxation. Slaveholders would have the power to prevent actions that hurt their interests. The small states gained a foothold in the Senate, the big states majority rule in the House, and the slave states the likelihood that they would benefit from majority rule.

The next eleven days of discussion about the committee's recommendations seemed to prove Madison right in another sense, however: the fault lines now really were more about slavery than about size. A dissatisfied Paterson tried to untie the logic of the compromise by pointing out that there was nothing democratic about representing chattel who neither voted nor were represented in their own states. He even raised the stakes, in the manner of the Congress's July 1776 debate, by observing that the extra representation for slaves would encourage the slave trade. He was answered by Madison, who pointed out the hypocrisy in Paterson's speaking out for the accurate representation of citizens by the federal government while advocating the representation of the states as equal. Madison still thought his earlier compromise of slaves counting for one house and not another to be much better. But it was just another unwieldy way of balancing interests, one that may have had less appeal because of its very frankness about slavery.

The principle of balance and compromise was winning. In this sense, slavery occupied the center of the first great compromise because it was so easy to recognize as a specific interest. It could be isolated more easily than the distinct powers of the states and the federal government, and quantified more easily than state size, the value of land, or sectional balance. In a political sense, slavery remained difficult to speak about, but it had become good to trade with.

As the delegates argued about the precise numbers for each state in the House of Representatives, and whether to set the numbers or tie them to changing census returns, some also advocated, again, for tying taxation as well as representation to the three-fifths ratio. Wilson found three-fifths for representation less objectionable if linked also to taxation. Referring to the actions of the Congress in 1783, Rufus King of Massachusetts reminded those from the Deep South that eleven of thirteen states had already "agreed to consider Slaves in the apportionment of taxation; and taxation and Representation ought to go together." The South Carolinians continued to argue for more protection for their property and particular interests, and northern delegates continued to push back in debates that took up much of the second week of July. A few delegates defended three-fifths as "about right." More described it as a necessary compromise.

Along the way, though, Wilson, Gouverneur Morris, and other relatively nationalist or northern and state-oriented delegates began to make stronger and clearer antislavery statements. In notes for a possibly undelivered speech titled "Acting Before the World," which surely informed his other conversations with fellow delegates, John Dickinson asked, "What will be said of this new principle of founding a Right to govern Freemen on a power derived from Slaves . . . The omitting the *Word* will be regarded as an Endeavour to conceal a principle of which we are ashamed." For Dickinson, power and right had converged: "Every Importation of Slaves will increase the power of the state over others. This principle I wish to avoid." Speeches like these angered at least one previously quiet North Carolinian delegate enough that he threatened not to confederate without at least three-fifths representation. Randolph, the Virginian, took the softer tack, "lament[ing] that such a species of property existed. But as it did exist the holders of it would require this security" precisely *because* Northerners did not identify with slavery and talked of "excluding slaves altogether."[28]

Discussing representation and taxation had brought out antislavery sentiments. Those expressions became a reason to protect slavery. The more likely it became that slaves would add to representation, the more the representation question tended to sectionalize the delegates. The realization of representation's open-endedness in an expanding republic—populations do change—also contributed to sectional combat over slavery in the convention. What effect would new territories have? The question of the western territories, and of the census as a method of counting and apportioning seats, complicated matters further. Because of the tens of thousands who had poured into Kentucky, Tennessee, and the southern backcountry since 1776, it was widely assumed that slave country would grow faster than free country. If it did, three-fifths would matter more.

Suddenly the three-fifths clause did not have its slim majority anymore. Morris worried aloud "that N.C. S.C. and Georgia only will in a little time have a majority of the people of America." Butler reiterated the Deep South line, minus the Virginian apologetics: "The security the South[er]n States want is that their negroes, may not be taken from them, which some gentlemen within or without doors, have a very good mind to do." Clearly, the abolition societies as well as their fellow travelers in the Congress had been heard.[29]

The rhetoric had become heated, and sectional, with big-state nationalists participating as often and as vigorously as small-state delegates. Nevertheless, on July 12 the convention had voted to link apportionment, and thus the federal ratio, explicitly to any measures for direct taxation by the federal government. On the sixteenth the convention finally voted to accept the Grand Committee's compromise as a whole. What made possible the actual passage of the first great compromise of the Constitutional Convention, despite the renaissance of antislavery and sectional arguments? Convention members were very likely aware of debates going on in New York, at meetings of the Continental Congress, about the future of slavery under the proposed Northwest Ordinance. The ordinance provided rules for the admission of states north of the Ohio River. The ordinance banned slavery in the Northwest and included a fugitive-slave clause that later appeared, almost word for word, in the federal constitution.[30]

Some delegates had left the convention for the Congress in New York during the Fourth of July break. Others returned with information and huddled with delegates from New England and the Deep South on the evening of the eleventh. On August 8, a member of the Continental Congress wrote a letter that explained the ban on slavery in the Northwest by referring to the desire of Southerners not to compete with possible future growers of tobacco in the Ohio River valley, and "sev[era]l other political reasons." Madison's secretary and protégé, Edward Coles, remembered being told by Madison that

the distracting question of slavery was agitating and retarding the labours of both [the Congress and the convention], and led to conferences and intercommunications of the members, which resulted in a compromise by which the northern or anti-slavery portion of the country agreed to incorporate into the Ordinance and Constitution the provision to restore fugitive slaves; and this mutual and concurrent action was the cause of the similarity of the provision contained in both, and had its influence in creating the great unanimity by which the Ordinance passed, and also making the Constitution more acceptable to slaveholders.[31]

Legally speaking, the ban on slavery in the Northwest implied its protection in the Southwest. If a "compromise of 1787" occurred, it formed the first of the great line-drawing territorial compromises over slavery, while simultaneously making the Constitution itself possible. If the Congress helped the convention resolve its fragmentation over the representation question, it suggests that the first compromise of 1787 did more than initiate the process that continued with the Missouri Compromise and the Compromise of 1850. The process of compromise actually continued the domain of the Continental Congress and its periodic brokerage of slavery—something that is hard to square with the traditional dismissal of the Continental Congress as an inefficient body superseded in importance by the convention even as both met during the summer of 1787. However subtle or overt, the compromise of 1787 solidified the practice of deal making between increasingly self-aware sections defined by slavery.

The delegates to both bodies had learned to expect hard

bargaining and a recurrence of the issue of slavery whenever basic questions of power arose. After the sixteenth the convention moved on to the executive branch and the appointment of judges, only to find the same questions of representation slowing attempts to design the other two branches of government. Madison again led the way in pointing out how carefully powers had to be calibrated. Advocating the popular election of the president—rather than by the legislature—he noted that the strictly popular election of the president by counting all the votes in the country would give the northern states an advantage because "the right of suffrage was much more diffusive in the Northern than the Southern States; and the latter could have no influence in the election on the score of the Negroes." A system of electors representing each state, based on the three-fifths ratio, could solve that problem. Similarly, if the Senate appointed judges, the results might be undemocratic and skewed to the smaller and more numerous northern states. Instead, the president, filtered through the three-fifths ratio, would appoint judges to be confirmed by the Senate.[32]

With preliminary votes taken on these matters, the convention decided on July 21 to commit the Virginia Plan and the modifications that had been made to it to a drafting committee that would present a new document after an eleven-day recess. They did so only after hearing one more reminder from Charles Pinckney "that if the Committee should fail to insert some security to the Southern States ag[ain]st an emancipation of slaves, and taxes on exports, he sh[oul]d be bound by duty to his State to vote ag[ain]st their Report."[33] The first great compromise had secured slaveholder interests but without resolving how slavery itself would be governed. The compromise had also grown the government, raising the stakes for slavery as for everything else. The next round of deliberations, shifting to specific powers of the federal government, would be more frankly, and angrily, brokered through slavery.

The Committee on Detail went about its work boldly, especially where it concerned the slavery question. Its makeup made a key difference. The South Carolinian John Rutledge joined Edmund Randolph, James Wilson, and two New Englanders, Nathaniel Gorham and Oliver Ellsworth, who had participated in discussions about sectional compromise. Its report has been called a "monument to Southern craft and gall," even a hijacking of the Constitution for proslavery purposes.[34]

The committee's draft made its new concessions to slavery especially clear by linking the most important ones in the same article, which provided for what the legislative branch could—and in this case could not—do. In one sentence it banned taxes on exports and on "the migration or importation of such persons as the several States shall think proper to admit," adding, for good measure, that such "migration" could not be banned, either. The combination of goods as exports and persons as imports epitomized the planters' logic. If any delegate missed the implications, his sensitivity would be raised a few lines further down. The next clause forbade a "capitation" or head tax without a new census (a tax that, with the three-fifths clause, could at least indirectly tax slaves). The clause after that required a two-thirds majority for any "navigation act" regulating commerce, an emendation that first emerges in a draft in Rutledge's handwriting.[35]

These clauses seem to have been a further price paid for national supremacy—the stronger government envisioned by the Virginia Plan. The draft left no doubt about the sovereignty of national laws. It limited the federal government, as Pinckney had demanded, where it might touch on slavery. After the Committee on Detail had done its work, the great compromise looked different from how it had before to some of the northern delegates. Instead of just brokering power through representation, the new draft could double-hamstring foreign relations and national economic policy. For Rufus King, it amounted to a rewriting if not a repudiation of the compromise. He tried a new argument that had been heard in the Congress but not yet in the convention. A true national union should not be forbidden to deal with a "weakness"—slavery—that would "render defence more difficult." If it did, it should certainly be allowed to tax the source of that weakness, imported slaves and what they produced. The compromise no longer made any sense: "either slaves should not be represented, or exports should be taxable," and slave imports limited, perhaps at some specific future date.[36]

To the canny deal maker Roger Sherman, the evils of the slave trade had already been pushed off the table; only minor adjustments remained. But another strategist and deal broker, Gouverneur Morris, also saw the pseudo-compromise emerging out of committee as a different bargain altogether. He proposed undoing the deal on representation–something he had tried to do before the July 26 recess–because the new changes amounted to "upholding domestic slavery." Because of slavery, proportioning taxation to representation would lead to inequality between sections. The trade-off of federal direct taxation for slave representation, he said prophetically, would amount to nothing in so large a country, where direct taxes would be so hard to administer.

Morris and King had been among those who had voiced morally motivated antislavery sentiments before. They had also both acquiesced in the compromises over slavery. What spurred their August 8 antislavery revival was a realization that both economic policy and power had shifted toward the South and slavery. If the plantation South's exports could not be taxed, if its slave imports became tax-free, and if commerce itself could not be regulated, that left two alternative modes of taxation. One was the kind of excise and local taxes on production and consumption that had caused Shays's Rebellion. The other was a tax on imports, a direct drain on the shipping interests of Boston, New York, and Philadelphia, whose merchants King and Morris represented.[37]

Sherman, Wilson, and Pinckney beat back this antislavery challenge with some minor and not very convincing objections. Evidently, the other delegates were not ready to forsake what they had already accomplished and enter into a new debate about political economy. The convention moved on to other aspects of the Committee on Detail draft, working through it clause by clause, postponing a full discussion of taxing exports when it first came up on August 16. When the question recurred on the twenty-first, however, the new clauses on exports, trade laws, and slave importation, because of their proximity as clauses, had to be considered in full and together—and the fur began to fly again in discussions that went on for most of the next two days.

The debate began as a matter of sections and economics. To avoid an explicit recurrence of the slavery issue, Pierce Butler even referred to the interests of the "Staple-States," as George Mason had done first when advocating for a ban on export taxes on the sixteenth (only to have Rutledge blow things open by calling attention to the "subsequent part relating to negroes"). The power to tax exports remained a major tool of state in the age of mercantilism. Even some of the localists, like John Dickinson, could not see restricting the federal government in this way. For others, especially George Mason, the issue remained fundamental, a question of whether the convention should be "reducing the States to mere corporations," as well as a question of whether the South could still be outvoted in the Congress and, as a result, potentially oppressed. When Madison, who spoke out as a nationalist in favor of state power to tax exports, suggested the two-thirds majority for such laws as a compromise, he lost. Massachusetts and Connecticut joined with a solid South to ban the export tax when the convention voted (unusually) on only that part of the clause.[38]

The next part, of course, was the special ban on taxing or prohibiting slave imports. Luther Martin, the voluble champion of small-state interests, jumped in with a counterproposal. In defending it, he pulled no punches. The three-fifths clause would encourage the slave trade. Slave imports were a national issue, not a local one, because slavery weakened one part of the union that every part had to protect militarily. Worst of all, "it was inconsistent with the principles of the revolution and dishonorable to the American character to have such a feature in the Constitution."[39]

As the historian Jack N. Rakove observes, "eight of the next nine" speeches recorded by Madison came from the Connecticut, Massachusetts, and Deep South delegates, in defense of their new compromise.[40] Rutledge answered first, with three remarkable arguments that added up to nothing less (and nothing more) than the most skilled stonewalling the convention had yet witnessed.

First, he denied that any slaves would actually be imported merely because permission to import could not be prohibited by the federal government. Second, and more boldly, he insisted that he wasn't worried about slave revolts and that the South did not need any help defending itself: something that had not been true during the Revolutionary War and that no other delegate ever dared say before or afterward. Finally, he refused to even pick up the antislavery gauntlet laid down by the Marylander Luther Martin. He did not attempt to defend slavery at all. Instead, he acknowledged that slavery was a matter of principle, only to make principle irrelevant to politics:

> Religion & humanity had nothing to do with this question. Interest alone is the governing principle with

nations. The true question at present is whether the South[er]n States shall or shall not be parties to the Union. If the Northern States consult their interest, they will not oppose the increase of Slaves which will increase the commodities of which they will become the carriers.[41]

The New England–Deep South alliance had been laid bare. The second compromise of 1787 had bargained the slave trade for a limited power over economic policy, minus the power to tax exports. Connecticut's Oliver Ellsworth embellished the deal by appealing to states' rights: the old confederation, he intoned, "had not meddled with this point," conveniently forgetting the bans on slave imports in 1774 and 1776. Pinckney, getting increasingly comfortable in his role as the Deep South's velvet glove, speculated that, left alone, South Carolina might just end the slave trade anyway, as Rutledge had hinted. (His cousin General Charles Pinckney, who prized his reputation for honesty, later said he didn't think so, but the disinformation damage had been done.) Sherman, never one to miss a rhetorical opportunity, picked up on the suggestion and gave "the good sense of the several States" the credit for the anti-slave-trade trend that would "probably" continue.

George Mason, a Virginian who cared as much about principle as anyone in the room, would have none of this claptrap. Slavery was "a whole Union" question. He took the Jeffersonian ground that he had helped develop during the 1760s. The British had introduced slavery and prevented its limitation; then they had tried to arm slaves during the war. Since then, Maryland, Virginia, and North Carolina had prohibited slave importation—but it would all be in vain if the "western people" were restocked by cheap imports coming through Georgia and South Carolina. Slavery discouraged manufacturing, lowered wages, and turned masters into "tyrants." Many state rights had already been given up, so why not this one? Like Luther Martin, he took the higher patriotic ground: "Providence punishes national sins, by national calamities."[42]

The Yankee-Carolina alliance refused to give much ground to nationalist antislavery arguments coming from erstwhile defenders of state powers like Mason and Martin. The unctuous Oliver Ellsworth was the first to accuse them of hypocrisy. If slavery was wrong, why not free all the slaves instead of just banning the trade? What is most striking about Ellsworth, Pinckney, and their allies is that their replies to antislavery criticisms of the second great compromise constitute a kind of one-two punch that, taken together, was far more inconsistent than anything their critics said, yet seem reasonable precisely because they emerged in different accents. Slavery was wrong, said the Yankees—but that didn't matter, because it was practiced the world over, added the Carolinians. The other Pinckney pointed out that with a ban on slave imports, Mason's Virginia would end up the supplier of surplus slaves to the West (not that he thought there was anything wrong with that). If arguments mattered—and with so many close votes, there is every reason to think they did—the second compromise of 1787 was forged in contradiction and won by a rhetorical strategy of divide and conquer.

At least until more Northerners stood up. Wilson hesitantly observed that to exempt only slavery from import taxes meant nothing less than a "bounty on that article." Dickinson, Gerry, and John Langdon of New Hampshire, each a defender of state privileges, all rose to agree with Mason that the slave trade remained a national question. With Carolinians maintaining that their states would never join a union with a slave-trade ban, Dickinson denied the truth of that political prediction.[43] Rufus King stressed that Northerners would be just as angry if the slave trade continued.

In response, the genteel nationalists on both sides of the question, including Pinckney, Edmund Randolph, and Gouverneur Morris, began to suggest the necessity of yet another formal deal-making process. A committee of eleven members, including Madison and some of the leaders of the debate, spent the evenings of August 22 and 23 developing language that, they hoped, would get approval by a majority.

They returned with a proposal that forbade a ban on the slave trade before 1800 and permitted a tax on "migration or importation" no higher than an average of existing import taxes. When the proposal came to the floor, General Pinckney moved to push back the permission to end the slave trade until 1808.

Madison was disturbed. Although he had not recorded speeches of his own during this round of debates, this time he bothered to write down his ideas on the subject. "Twenty years will produce all the mischief that can be apprehended from the liberty to import slaves," he insisted. "So long a term will be more dishonorable to the National character than to say nothing about it in the Constitution." The change to 1808 passed anyway, opposed by Franklin and other lower-north and upper-south delegates but receiving decisive yea votes from the Deep South, Maryland, and New England. Madison succeeded only in getting through a semantic change, agreed to by Sherman of Connecticut, that kept the slave-trade clause from stating directly "that there could be property in men." Instead, the clause ultimately allowed a tax "not exceeding ten dollars for each person," a change that obscured its purpose, making it sound as if it concerned free immigrants rather than slaves at all.[44]

What Pinckney called the "liberality" shown especially by the New Englanders toward the slave trade motivated a majority of Carolinians formally to give in on the rule of a special two-thirds majority in the legislature for commercial regulation. Butler called it a concession he was willing to make to win "the affections of the East[ern] States." Rutledge, who had first inserted the supermajority for commercial regulation into the Committee on Detail report, now waxed profound and nationalist in supporting commercial regulation: "As we are laying the foundation of a great empire, we ought to take a permanent view of the subject and not look at the present moment only." The convention proceeded to strike out the entire navigation-act clause. Butler immediately proposed the addition of the fugitive-slave clause modeled on the clause in the new Northwest Ordinance. It passed unanimously.[45]

By the end of August the federal constitutional consensus had emerged clearly enough for all the delegates to see. Slavery would be protected by several interlocking provisions—but not mentioned explicitly. The federal government would be strengthened, but with exceptions that would decrease the likelihood of any region's predominance, and especially any move against southern institutions. The move toward careful euphemism informed the revision of the militia clause on August 31: too obviously suggestive of slavery, the federal government's guarantee of protection against "domestic violence" became simply "insurrections."

A proposal from Madison setting procedures for constitutional amendments and their ratification by the states passed after the addition of one crucial exception, demanded by John Rutledge, who "said he could never agree to give a power by which the articles relating to slaves might be altered by the States not interested in that property and prejudiced against it." Instead, an exception to the amendment clause was built in: the Constitution could be amended before 1808 in any manner that did not affect the slave-trade clause. This was accomplished by referring to the article in question, not by mentioning the slave trade. Similarly, in the three-fifths clause, "bound to Service" substituted for "servitude" because, as Edmund Randolph insisted, it more clearly suggested slaves rather than indentured servants but without saying so. And in the fugitive-slave clause, the delegates dropped the term "legally" from the phrase "legally held to service in one state," because, according to Madison, it would have implied a commitment to the legality of slavery in general.[46]

Madison had said his piece; now he wanted to cover the convention's tracks and hope for the best. The modern name for these late moves on the part of the delegates is damage control. The damage in question was the potential backlash coming from Americans who opposed slavery. The compromises of 1787 rankled before the ink was dry, and they did not go unchallenged. George Mason and Elbridge Gerry, two of the more eminent delegates, painfully and movingly expressed their opposition to the finished product during the convention's waning days. Mason worried about the expansive powers of the Congress in light of the lack of a check on navigation acts, and feared that as a result the Constitution would never be ratified. He made a last-ditch effort to include the two-thirds majority for a navigation act in the slave-trade clause, but his proposal was turned down. In seeking to resuscitate the navigation act and combine it with the slave-trade compromise, Mason made it clear, on the last day of the convention, that he saw this flaw as inseparable from the suspicious deal concerning the slave trade.

Mason's initial draft of objections to the Constitution, which he distributed to friends soon after the convention, began by dissecting the possibilities for the oppression of the states, of individuals, and of the South under the new government, and ended with the failure to allow the government to restrict the slave trade. For Mason, the slave-trade compromise remained the root cause of the problems. He later remarked to Jefferson that the draft constitution had been one he could have signed until the bargain of Carolina and Georgia "with the three New England States . . . Under this coalition, the great principles of the Constitution were changed in the last days of the Convention."

Elbridge Gerry fingered the three-fifths clause as a fatal flaw in the Constitution. He said he could "get over" this and other objections were it not for the fearsome powers of the federal government.[47] His dissent paralleled Mason's in insisting that slavery-related provisions reflected and contributed to problems in the larger structure of the federal government. The critiques launched by these two important delegates shaped and emboldened antifederalist attacks on the Constitution. And they certainly disprove the notion that it is "anachronistic" or politically correct to consider how slavery affected other aspects of the founders' great design.[48] Surely we can ask the same questions if delegates were doing so before the convention ended. What, finally, was the place of slavery in the Constitution the framers produced?

The clauses that relate directly to slavery are not exceptions to the Constitution's remarkable combination of precision and vagueness: they epitomize those qualities. The founders' Constitution simultaneously evades, legalizes, and calibrates slavery, as it does so much else, including its very raison d'être, the creation of a stronger federal republic. No more than it does slavery, the Constitution does not mention nationhood—for fear of offending the localists—rendering it all the more an ideal national charter for soft selling its version of a modern nation-state.

It is common, and accurate enough, to say that the federal republic could not have been created in 1787–88 had not slavery been left alone, but the convention went further and deeper than that. In the founders' design, slavery informed the successes of the movement for a stronger national government and shaped its limits. Because proslavery forces were able to make deals to protect their interests in particular, slavery itself gained the protection of the federal union while being protected from that union's new powers. Insofar as the federalist movement and the convention created another Mansfieldian moment, slavery survived that moment through the balancing of interests in an artful design. Which is to say, the framers turned their Mansfieldian moment into "the Madisonian moment."[49]

The compromises of 1787 welded together two dimensions of the politics of slavery: slavery as a form of governance over certain people, and slavery as an economic institution. Even to contemplate, much less codify, this much governance, and that much economic regulation, was itself risky after a revolution against imperial governance and regulation. In the end, the founders used slavery to limit government while allowing slaves to be governed both locally and nationally. In fewer, smaller ways, slavery was itself limited. More decisively, slavery was alternately winked at and silenced as a subject of political debate and adjudication. In the process, it was not so much forgotten as contained.

In the Constitutional Convention, American politics had indeed become a culmination of the American Revolution: an officially slavery-free zone of debate predicated on, and at critical moments obsessed with, slavery. It was not that slavery "failed to engage the creative energies of the founders in their fullest form or was inherently unsoluble," as Joseph J. Ellis suggests.[50] Instead, the founders' creative energies had turned disagreement, even contradiction, regarding slavery into a structure to manage doubts and conflicts about nationhood as well as slavery itself. The business of slavery had not been left unfinished so much as it had been leveraged.[51]

In closing the convention, key proslavery and antislavery delegates like Charles Cotesworth Pinckney and Gouverneur Morris turned the deals, and the ambiguities, into virtues. In light of requests by Randolph, Mason, and Gerry for a second convention, Pinckney said that the delegates should project unanimity in order to get the document ratified. Morris, who had challenged Southerners on slavery as much as anyone, promised to follow the decisions of the majority, for the real question was whether a national government would in fact result from their hard work. Franklin put it most eloquently: "The opinions I have had of its errors, I sacrifice to the public good." Who could say this constitution was not the best human hands could make? Ultimately, good government depended on the humans who administered it, and the people who earned good or despotic rule. "If every one of us in returning to our Constituents were to report the objections he has had to it, and endeavor to gain partizans in support of them, we might prevent its being generally received, and thereby lose all the salutary effects & great advantages resulting naturally in our favor among foreign Nations as well as among ourselves, from our real or apparent unanimity."[52]

The printer and diplomat Franklin knew that the appearance of unanimity could create the reality. Perception and public opinion mattered as much as the deals and the details. Silence and compromise became virtues. In this remark Franklin justified not only his own mediating role in the convention but also his silence about slavery, epitomized by his decision not to present the Pennsylvania Abolition Society's petition against the slave trade. Hamilton had made a similar choice with the New York society's petition, and he probably had even more objections to the finished document than Franklin did. In the wake of these virtuous silences, the original fire bell in the night that threatened to undo the union became not only slavery itself but also, as Ellis writes, "the act of talking publicly about slavery."[53] The question of ratification, then, would consist in part of whether the citizenry could follow the convention's lead and talk about slavery in ways that advanced the kind of "liberality" epitomized by Franklin, Pinckney, and Morris.

In its last act before signing the Constitution, the convention deposited its records with George Washington. They chose well. Washington had led the way to the convention, presided over it, and made it clear throughout that there could be "no greater evil than disunion." Washington proceeded to freeze out his good friend and neighbor George Mason for opposing the Constitution. But he did not deceive himself about what had happened. Soon after the convention, he began to express new regrets about slavery and decided to set an example by emancipating his own slaves in his will.[54] That President Washington decided that slavery was wrong yet felt bound by the Constitution to do nothing about it captures the main effects that the Constitution had on slavery and American politics. The framers' Constitution disapproved of slavery by implication but made it harder to do much about it nationally. After all, the people's natural leaders had done their best. This was slavery republicanized—and depoliticized. It remained to be seen what would happen when the people themselves had a say.

THREE

Protesting and Ratifying Slavery's Constitution

In September 1787, the people had not yet spoken. The Constitution had to be ratified by the people's representatives in the states to achieve legitimacy as the law of the land. Especially because it had been written and debated behind closed doors, the Constitution had to be justified and explained out of doors—in the press and in the streets.

Even though the convention did an end run around the Continental Congress, in its procedure, membership, and even location the convention had very much resembled the Congress. Ratification, by contrast, only partly resembled electoral politics in the states. Because constitutional ratification occurred in the states, but in reference to events going on elsewhere, in an electoral process both sequential and simultaneous, it became something else: the beginnings of American national politics. Local and national at once, the process of ratification has as much to tell us as the convention does about the place of slavery in that politics.

[handwritten: constitution = beginning of American national politics → constitution tells us about the place of slavery in politics]

Critics of the Constitution quickly perceived the compromises of 1787. Somewhat more gradually, they developed ideas about what those compromises indicated about the rest of the framers' design. As antislavery became a significant, if not ubiquitous, theme in the debate over the Constitution during the fall and winter, federalists were forced to respond. North of Virginia, they developed four main justifications, or excuses, for the place of slavery in the Constitution. They celebrated compromise. They admitted the presence of necessary evils. They projected blame onto the Deep South. And they exaggerated the Constitution's antislavery implications.

During the ratification debates, more framers, like the authors of *The Federalist*, went public with their disavowals of slavery, in order to help get the Constitution passed by majority votes in key state conventions. Yet the state-by-state nature of ratification made it easier for the federalists to stress different, even contradictory, aspects of the Constitution to different constituencies. The responses on the local level, and the rebuttals offered by the framers and their allies, established a pattern for the volatile mix of slavery, constitutionalism, and American party politics in the nineteenth century.

Antislavery, in its antifederalist mode, ultimately lost in the struggle for ratification, as antislavery would lose repeatedly in mainstream politics for the next several generations thanks in part to the Constitution's rules. Its localism, in the end, was its great strength and its fatal weakness in a struggle against a nationalist silencing of the slavery issue. Still, antifederalist criticisms of slavery's Constitution—and especially arguments about

how compromises over slavery reflected and papered over related political problems—were heard. Antislavery politics gained
publicity, credibility, and further refinement. Some antifederalists even called the framers on their selective federalism: their
willingness to allow slavery in particular to escape from the over-
sight of the nation-state. Thanks to the antifederalists' doomed
struggle against the Constitution, antislavery became part of an
American tradition of dissent.

Foreign ministers were especially struck by the "infinite amount
of writing pro and con" during the fall and winter ratification
debates. After two months of watching federalists and antifederalists abuse each other "with a rancor which sometimes does not
even spare insults and personal invectives," Louis-Guillaume
Otto, the French chargé d'affaires in Philadelphia, wrote home
that the process itself had changed the political landscape. Cries
of crisis from both sides had just about destroyed the reputation
of the federal government. With the French Revolution still over
the horizon, Otto could only shake his head at such domestic
navel-gazing. Ironically, "it was impossible to carry out a more
violent coup to the authority of Congress, than in saying to all
America . . . that this body is inadequate to the needs of the
Confederation and that the United States have become the
laughingstock of all the powers. This principle repeated over and
over by all the Innovators seems as false as their spirits are
excited," Otto insisted. Even if we discount for Otto's diplomatic
perspective and his French preference for the United States to

remain a client state rather than a new empire, Otto perceived something essential, and in a sense absurd, about what came to be called the "grand national discussion" of 1787–88. In ratifying the Constitution, Americans were not solely or even mainly fixing the ability of their state to conduct external relations and protect the economy, even though these were arguably the most important tasks at hand. They were holding something like a referendum on the Revolution and the future.[1]

The Federalists began with some powerful advantages. The convention had projected consensus. While the convention met, printers who lacked actual information tended to publish vague praise for the gathering of great men in Philadelphia, many of whom had become famous by 1787. Even Thomas Jefferson prefaced his critique of the convention's secrecy by calling it "an assembly of demigods." Readers of American newspapers, most of which were published in seaport towns where concerns about the economy predominated, could hardly be faulted for assuming what most textbooks still tell us: that the worthy delegates, led by Washington and Franklin, had convened just in time to save the Republic from ruin. If only because of their very worthiness, what they came up with would seem likely to be an improvement upon recent experience.[2]

Given the focus, then and ever since, on the greatness of the founders, it is hard for us to imagine that opponents of the Constitution ever had a chance, much less an argument.[3] Consequently, it is even harder for us to remember the fact that the antifederalists, as the founders labeled them, almost won the debate over ratification in late 1787–88. Ratification, unlike laws passed by the Continental Congress, became official when nine (rather than all thirteen) of the states voted for it in convention. Even this took nine months. Virginia and New York, the biggest states, were among the holdouts. Early setbacks in North Carolina and Rhode Island made those states seem highly unlikely to agree to the Constitution unless threatened with being left out of a viable union otherwise. Halfway through the anxious months, on February 6, 1788, the vote to approve was dangerously close (184 to 168) in Massachusetts, the seedbed of the Revolution but also the site of Shays's Rebellion. Only a promise of amendments (and possibly some other backstage deal) convinced a few key leaders like John Hancock to switch sides.

Then the process stalled, with seven of thirteen states undecided. No states ratified between February 6 and April 26 (Maryland). What can explain the extended, nail-biting drama of ratification, the drama we have mostly forgotten in favor of the Philadelphia convention? First of all, antifederalists did have some real advantages in debating the merits of the document. The Constitution created a new, arguably distant, supreme national government, even if its supporters tried to play up their "federalism." The convention had exceeded its mandate, bespeaking a "we the people" where none had, legally, existed. When antifederalists stood with the states, and championed local control, they emphasized institutions that had fought the Revolution and preserved traditional liberties. A national government, even a federal one, that put coordination before local prerogative smelled like the British Empire after the Seven Years' War. Americans over the age of, say, forty sometimes found it hard to forget that the Revolution had been fought to stymie, not create, an imperial administration.

To equate imperial tyranny with a federal structure that had not yet been tried struck many federalists as paranoid, but such paranoia had motivated the resistance movement and the militia during the war. In rural areas, some believed that the state governments were already insufficiently responsive to the needs of local people, especially with respect to taxation and the economy. They wanted more democracy and local power, not less. To these folks, the schemes of planters, merchants, and lawyers sounded like more of the same: another way to "new model" the government to take power away from ordinary people. The federalists had creative political thinking, enthusiasm for nationhood, and imperial dreams on their side. The antifederalists had the republican tradition and the resisting soul of the Revolution. The Constitution gave them something else to resist.

Compromise has its virtues but also its limitations. The presumption that the people themselves should contemplate, discuss, and ratify the Constitution through their representatives in convention presupposed the active use of reason and criticism. To rush the process of ratification under presumption of a crisis, as Federalists did successfully in Pennsylvania and Delaware, suggested ulterior motives. The secrecy that had allowed for frank debate and creative deals in convention could be—and quickly was—reinterpreted as conspiratorial and undemocratic. The Pennsylvanian Samuel Bryan, writing as "Centinel" in one of the first important and widely reprinted antifederalist essays, captured this sensibility in his chosen pen name. "Our situation is represented to be so *critically* dreadful, that, however reprehensible and exceptionable the proposed plan of government may be, there is no alternative, between the adoption of it and absolute ruin," he wrote in his first piece, published on October 5. This "argument of tyrants" contrasted with what true republican centinels should do: warn the people to carefully consider every article and clause for the potential threat they presented to their liberties.[4]

For antifederalists like Bryan, process was substance. Debate epitomized and guarded liberty. The federalist rush to ratify reeked of conspiracy. Such concerns about process could only be answered in debate.

What implications did this understanding of process have for the place of slavery in the ratification struggle? On the one hand, the framers had artfully hidden the evidence of compromise and even the subject itself in silence and ambiguity. A quick ratification would, in effect, ratify the decision not to unpack the ambiguities or spell out the compromises. Constitutions make rules, but tough legal decisions of all kinds tend to rely on what the legal scholar Cass Sunstein has called "incompletely theorized agreements" that "enlist silence" in order to achieve "agreements on results and low level principles amid confusion or dissensus" on fundamentals.[5] The founders' Constitution avoided theorizing African slavery as right or wrong, as an Old World holdover or a New World innovation, as a pillar of the Republic or an anachronism headed for the dustbin of history, as something that could be legislated or something that could not, because they could not agree on these things. The text they enshrined allowed for different possible results: slavery's continuance, spread, or eventual end.

At the same time—and this is ultimately what makes the document proslavery—the Constitution enacted mechanisms that empowered slaveholders politically, which would prevent the national government from becoming an immediate or likely impediment to the institution. The most clear "low level" principle resolved was that the issue ought to be avoided in the normal course of national political debate and action—that is, silence itself—and that the Constitution itself embodied a legitimate, reasoned, fairly determined compromise. The "result" agreed to was slavery's continuance and protection in the present and near future. This made the Constitution nominally neutral but operationally proslavery.

During ratification strikingly few people in the Deep South criticized the Constitution for being insufficiently proslavery. Where slavery's protection was an overriding issue, in other words, the dominant planter classes were satisfied by what the convention had produced. The relative absence of debate on the topic in North Carolina, South Carolina, and Georgia speaks volumes. There was little hand-wringing about whether a deal over slavery had occurred or not and whether such deals made the larger package suspect. Rather, the deal made the bargain worthwhile, especially for those from planter-dominated districts. Georgia ratified quickly and unanimously. The only reason North Carolina did not ratify was because slavery-dominated districts did not outnumber those where small farmers predominated.[6]

In South Carolina, the legislature debated the Constitution in January 1788 before deciding whether to hold elections for a convention. Rawlins Lowndes raised the possibility of sectional domination through majority rule in the Congress, and cited northern interest in legislating the slave trade as a portent of things to come. But the Rutledges and the Pinckneys used their inside knowledge to argue that in fact they had made a fine bargain and retained a preponderance of power for planters. Population growth would add to southern representation; Charles Cotesworth Pinckney added, "I did not expect that . . . we had conceded too much to the Eastern States, when they allowed us a representation for a specie of property which they have not among them." General Charles Pinckney also defended the second great compromise as a great deal, considering that "the Middle States and Virginia" had wanted to end the slave trade permanently, and "we have obtained a right to recover our slaves in whatever part of America they may take refuge, which is a right we had not before." A better deal could not have been had. When the South Carolina convention finally met in May, the disproportionately represented low-country districts, with the highest proportion of slaves, voted federalist, ratifying the Constitution by a vote of 149 to 73.[7]

By contrast, northern critics of the Constitution brought up the issue early, and surprisingly often. It is tempting to dismiss antifederalist antislavery as cynical or insincere—an appeal to sectional animosity by committed localists—as neither pure nor "really" about slavery.[8] If we do so, we impose our single-issue understanding of slavery on the past, and in the process we miss something important about what the antifederalists knew, and what they were for as well as against. Opponents of the Constitution understood that the federal government created in Philadelphia was an open-ended compact that made key concessions to Southerners, could evolve in various directions, and might have different implications in different circumstances. It might well work to decrease the ability of the people—locally or nationally—to end slavery. More than ever before, after the Constitution slavery seemed to be connected to everything else. The Constitution's dealings with slavery, in short, reflected the very power shifts, and ambiguities, that worried antifederalists.

Most major antifederalist writers—such as Centinel, Cato, and Brutus—turned to the slavery issue during the fall months, highlighting the three-fifths clause, the slave trade, and other implications of slavery in the Constitution. In this they followed, as well as advanced, the word on the street. The Reverend William Bentley of Salem, Massachusetts, who prided himself on talking to everybody, recorded in his diary on October 3 that "some complaint is made that the advantage is unduly thrown in favor of the representation from the Southern States, &c &c."[9] A satirical list of "blessings" of the Constitution offered up in a Philadelphia newspaper on November 14 included "Free importation of negroes for one and twenty years." Federalists read enough such material in Pennsylvania that one replied with a recipe for a formulaic antifederalist screed:

> WELL-BORN, nine times—*Aristocracy*, eighteen times—
> *Liberty of the Press*, thirteen times repeated—*Liberty of Con-*

science, once—*Negroe slavery*, once mentioned—*Trial by jury*, seven times—*Great Men*, six times repeated—*Mr. Wilson*, forty times—and lastly, GEORGE MASON'S *Right Hand in a Cutting-box*, nineteen times—put them all together, and dish them up with pleasure.

The mock recipe gets the function that slavery played in antifederalism nearly right. Slavery did not take up many column inches. It did not have to be repeated ad nauseam in order to be a crucial ingredient mixed in at the appropriate moment. One pinch of a powerful substance can change the nature of the dish. Those with an appetite whetted by reading the papers would know that James Wilson had justified the concessions to slaveholders, and that George Mason had said he'd give up his right hand rather than sign on to them.[10]

Leading writers like Samuel Bryan appear to have realized during October and November 1787 that the ways slavery inhabited the Constitution actually strengthened their overall case against its aristocratic, insufficiently republican, and possibly deceitful character. As a result, they worked slavery into their other arguments—not to downplay it or to cynically overplay it, but to express their sense of how slavery typified the Constitution's tightly interwoven problems.

Bryan, a committed abolitionist, overlooked slavery in his quickly turned-out and widely reprinted first two Centinel essays, even though he briefly considered the question of representation in them. But by early November he had connected the dots. The Constitution guaranteed a republican form of government to the states—but didn't its protections for slavery undermine republican government as well? The security for the slave trade in Article I, Section 9, he wrote, went against what other states had already done to purify themselves of slavery's corruption, and "is especially scandalous and inconsistant in a people, who have asserted their own liberty by the sword, and which dangerously enfeebles the districts, wherein the laborers are bondsmen. The words are dark and ambiguous; such as no plain man of common sense would have used, [and] are evidently chosen to conceal from Europe, that in this enlightened country, the practice of slavery has its advocates among men in the highest stations." The Constitution partook of propaganda. The corollary: don't trust men in the highest stations. Then Bryan immediately turned to the economic implications. Three-fifths of the slaves would be represented, but no poll tax on them would be allowed to burden their owners, and the impost on their consumption would be negligible. His conclusion: the participation of five southern states had been "purchased too dearly." This was no way to relaunch a republic.[11]

In early October, Federal Farmer (Melancton Smith of New York) tied the unwieldy nature of the proposed federal union to the dominance of slaveholders in the South. A month later, he described the South as having been bought off by having its slaves represented. Likewise, Brutus attacked the three-fifths clause directly and at length in his third essay on November 15, calling it an outrageous attempt to conceal a backlash against Revolutionary principles, including the granting of "unreasonable weight in the government" to the slave South. The pass

3/5
compromise·
blackism of
revolutionary
principles

stated in Constitution

given the slave trade added insult to the injury, creating a political incentive to enslave more Africans.[12]

Brutus's attack on slavery's presence in the Constitution comes immediately before his often-quoted theory of representation, in which representatives must resemble the people they represent: "They are the sign—the people are the thing signified." The vast number of people to be represented by each congressman typified the "merely nominal," undemocratic nature of representation under the Constitution. Cato (probably George Clinton), another New Yorker, echoed this criticism, stating even more directly that trucking with Southerners allowed slavery to corrupt representation, the heart of republican government. To give more power to Southerners was to hand the federal government over to the least egalitarian people in the United States.[13]

And who else would try to establish the slave trade for twenty more years after most of the states, and the Continental Congress, had moved against it? Agrippa (James Winthrop of Massachusetts) looked to climate for an explanation of southern political behavior. "The inhabitants of warmer climates are more dissolute in their manners, and less industrious, than in colder countries. A degree of severity is, therefore, necessary." If "it is impossible for one code of laws to suit Massachusetts and Georgia," Northerners needed to legislate for themselves. Would they be allowed to do so under the new constitution? Power in consolidated empires tended to migrate from the peripheries to the center. The most systematic northern dissectors of the Constitution, like Winthrop, stood on solid, traditional ground in declaring that "the very great empires have always been despotick."[14]

Southern vital for economy

What was new was to associate such imperial despotism with African slavery and the southern interest.

Benjamin Workman of Philadelphia, a College of Philadelphia instructor writing as "Philadelphiensis," expressed shock that so many Pennsylvania Quakers, putatively abolitionist, supported the Constitution. With no law guaranteeing religious liberties, what would prevent Philadelphia militiamen from being forced to bear arms against slave rebels in Georgia? Anyone subjected to such a compulsion would be, in effect, enslaved, "more to be pitied . . . than the wretches against whom he is compelled to fight!" Workman did not neglect to wish slave rebels "success in their first attempt." He was far from the only antifederalist to notice the implications of the insurrections clause. The officially antislavery stance of his state, and the embrace of federalism by many Quaker abolitionists, placed him out in front rhetorically and freed him to accuse the local federalists of betrayal. Only greed, and lust for power, could explain how "the professed enemies of *negro* and every other species of slavery, should themselves join in the adoption of a constitution whose very basis is *despotism* and *slavery*."[15]

During the autumn months, two old patriots—Benjamin Gale of Connecticut and Hugh Hughes of New York—wrote speeches and essays that went beyond invocations of the three-fifths clause, the slave trade, and sectional difference and placed slavery at the center of an analysis of the forces that reminded them of British attempts to strip the colonists of their liberties. While it is hard to say how influential these men were, they seem to have represented a growing sense among antifederalists

120

that a constitution that risked their property and their political power added up to a prospect of enslavement—the same sort of enslavement they had denounced since the 1760s. The proslavery dimensions of the Constitution, along with the Constitution's opacity where it concerned slavery, epitomized these tendencies, and evoked in these writers a special kind of shock, anger, and eloquence.

The ardently pro-federalist *Connecticut Courant* refused to print Gale's essay against the Constitution, so he had his say at a town meeting in Killingworth on November 12. Imagine a seventy-two-year-old sometime doctor and mill operator standing up and denouncing the proposed constitution as the most *"dark, intricate, crafty and unintelligible composition that I ever read or see composed by man."* The craftiness, and the rashly called elections for delegates to the convention, revealed the true origins of the Constitution in "the artful schemes of *designing men* who would recover their commutation securities and the notes purchased of the soldiers." Gale foresaw a large bureaucracy of federal "revenue officers" who would have to be paid gentleman's salaries in the South, where such men "have 3, 4, 5, and six hundred slaves of their own, have high notions of things, and can bet more on a horse race than the value of one of our little farms." The expense alone would "crush common people into the dust and reduce them to a state of vassalage and slavery." And why not? Slaveholders did not know any better, having "no idea but that our day laborers may be treated just as they treat their African slaves."

States with slaves had more votes in the Congress than

states without them, making the three-fifths clause reason enough to reject the document. Gale also perceived a special moral taint in the slave-trade clause, especially in its use of "sly cunning and artful" euphemism to hide its offense against "the rights of human nature." Nevertheless, it was all of a piece. There would be no need to extend the slave trade for twenty-one years or half that time: sooner than that, "3/4 of us will be slaves to all intents and purposes whatsoever without any trouble or expense of sending to Africa for slaves, for it is as perfect a system of slavery as I ever saw planned out by any nation, kingdom or state whatever. For what have we been contending and shedding our blood and wasting our substance, but to support the natural rights of men." Gale did not voice some new form of radicalism. In a region that had seen successive revolts over taxes, where people went to town meetings to vote on local appropriations and believed that the power to tax was the power to destroy, he spoke the language of experience as well as the language of the Revolution.[16]

Gale's townsmen elected him to the state ratifying convention. Were other such voices heard at town meetings? Did others so fully link the issues of local power and African slavery to highlight the risks of the new constitution? Did people listen? Some meetings in Massachusetts and New Hampshire forthrightly denounced the Constitution for its stance on slavery alone. One of them sent the Quaker minister John Neal to the Massachusetts convention, where he set perhaps the highest standard for moral critique by stating that Americans *deserved* to be enslaved if they agreed to a compact that legalized the slave trade. In rural areas, where few tangible economic incentives made the compromises of 1787 seem rational, and where people had reason to wonder whether the Constitution would empower them economically or politically, some made the link between slavery and their political disempowerment because the link made sense to them. It had been made and made again long before 1787.

Antifederalist antislavery received its fullest hearing at the New Hampshire and Massachusetts ratifying conventions. In New Hampshire, it contributed to federalists' push to postpone an actual vote from February to June. In Massachusetts, where the ratification convention also met in late January and early February, slavery was an important factor. The divisions in the state over taxation and power that had played out in Shays's Rebellion and the 1787 state elections informed the ratification debate. What some saw as necessary measures to revive the economy and pay debts others saw as schemes to create a new aristocracy. In late October, a writer in Boston's *Massachusetts Centinel* exulted that the Constitution itself would "diffuse a *national spirit*" and actually change people's sense of self; they would cease to be "merely the individual of a State, but a CITI-ZEN of AMERICA." This writer revealed a basic difference of perspective from opponents of the Constitution, who perceived local and state attachments *as* citizenship, not mere individuality. Little wonder that they heard in such federalist exultations the distinct possibility of a political shell game. Rufus King was worried enough to write Madison that "our prospects are gloomy."[17]

Antifederalist traditionalists, like the twenty-one-year-old

John Quincy Adams, feared the loss of "a System I have always been taught to cherish." They were not mollified when federalists told them to get with the nationalist-imperialist program. Some federalists were just as tone-deaf to the meanings of slavery as they had been to the implications of tax payments in hard coin to pay the interest on bonds held by speculators. One confident prognosticator insisted that opponents of the Constitution showed themselves to have a slave-like mentality when they insisted upon a charter of rights. Such charters were meant for feudal times—that is, an age of slavery—rather than a new era of self-government.

Given that the elected government of Massachusetts had just weathered a severe crisis of legitimacy and had called on outside troops to quell a tax revolt, only to have the people vote the administration out of office, the dawn of the new age of self-government lay in the eye of the beholder. The antifederalist James Warren preferred a more cyclical vision of history. To him, the three-fifths clause served as merely the new version of power's tendency to corrupt true representation, degrading the citizenry of Massachusetts "to the level of slaves." We might as well have accepted Parliament's "virtual representation" as this latter-day, southern version, Warren insisted.[18]

If the three-fifths clause distorted representation, it would inevitably warp the tax schemes adopted by the Congress, much as the dominance of merchant interests in Boston shaped the Massachusetts assembly's choice of revenue measures. The Congress would adopt poll taxes rather than excise or import taxes, further squeezing ordinary farmers. Sectional and antislavery concerns reinforced the local issues that had caused Shays's Rebellion and which, in turn, had motivated some Easterners to support the Constitutional Convention in the first place. Bostonians had called import and stamp taxes "slavery" during the 1760s, but Massachusetts farmers had joined the protests of Bostonians when the British government had sent troops and shut down their elected government. To these antifederalists, only the cast of characters, and the alliances against their liberties, had changed.[19]

True to script, urban interests—merchants and artisans, with the help of a few Continental army veterans like General William Heath—defended the Constitution's evident alliances in the Massachusetts convention. The Boston merchant John Hancock and the artisan spokesman Samuel Adams provided the key leadership and votes, even though they had begun the process as antifederalists. They helped "defuse the potentially explosive slavery issue" by declaring that the slave-trade clause allowed for eventual emancipation and by accepting the idea of ratification with recommended amendments. The recommended bill of rights passed by the Massachusetts convention included an amendment that would require the government to exhaust all other means of taxation before it turned to a poll tax. The Virginian Edmund Randolph understood this measure as an attack on southern interests and a result of the extended discussion of the slave power at the ratification convention.[20]

Federalists had a great deal to say about the identity of their opponents. The rural, and often western, grassroots opposition to the Constitution seemed to many articulate federalists to prove a point that Hamilton and Madison drove home in their Publius essays, collected later as *The Federalist*: that men who took a larger view of things needed to be filtered through the process of representation before being trusted with national affairs. In Massachusetts, opponents of the Constitution could smell the class connotations of this version of federalism a mile away. When supposedly provincial localists spoke the language of natural rights and antislavery, and in doing so claimed that the Constitution amounted to a rich men's conspiracy, it created a potent challenge to the entire federalist worldview, with its marriage of nationalism and uplift guided by a handful of wise founders.[21]

Three Massachusetts convention delegates felt compelled to return home to Hampshire County and publish their dissent in the local newspaper. There is no question that Consider Arms, Malachi Maynard, and Samuel Field were as provincially Yankee as their names suggest. Arms and Maynard had supported the Shaysites and later taken loyalty oaths. Yet by the time they wrote their dissent, they had decided that the best way to make their case about the problems with the Constitution was to highlight slavery and the betrayal of ideals by leaders in the state and nation.

To Field, Maynard, and Arms, the federal constitution directly contradicted the state constitution, which insisted, as did the Declaration, that "all men are born free and equal." Like Benjamin Gale, they asked what would keep them from being enslaved under a constitution that seemed to reject the basic principles of the Revolution. They also explicitly refused the

justification of skin color. Slavery was not about race: it was
about politics and power. Only sophistry and lucre could
explain the compromise of conscience involved when men who
had helped end African slavery in the state signed on to its survival in the nation.

Arms, Maynard, and Field reserved a special contempt for
the blame game and the selective reversion to localism they
heard from the federalists in convention. It had been said, "It is
not *we* doing it." To the contrary, insisted these quintessential
provincials, "We are the nation" who will have to defend slaveholders when "Africans rise up" and a foreign power intervenes
on their side. Why wasn't the prohibition of the slave trade by
the Continental Congress in 1774 an ironclad precedent? "Can
we suppose what was morally evil in the year 1774, has become
in the year 1788, morally good?" Perhaps tired of reading about
people like themselves as living proof of the need for better leadership, the dissenters turned their antifederalist antislavery into
a blast against the founders themselves.

> We cannot but say [that] the conduct of those who asso-
> ciated in the year 1774 in the manner above, and now
> appear advocates for the new constitution, is highly
> inconsistent, although we find such conduct has the cel-
> ebrated names of a *Washington* and an *Adams* to grace
> it . . . It was urged that the gentlemen who composed
> the federal Convention, were men of the greatest abili-
> ties, integrity and erudition, and had been the greatest
> contenders for freedom. We suppose it to be true, and

that they have exemplified it, by the manner, in which they have earnestly dogmatized for liberty—But notwithstanding we could not view this argument, as advancing any where towards infallibility—because long before we entered upon the business of the Convention, we were by some means or other possessed with a notion (and we think from good authority) that "*great men are not always wise*." And to be sure the weight of a name adduced to give efficacy to a measure where liberty is in dispute, cannot be so likely to have its intended effect, when the person designed by that name, at the same time he is brandishing his sword, in the behalf of freedom for himself—is likewise tyrannizing over two or three hundred miserable Africans, as free born as himself.[22]

The slavery clauses reflected more than a failure of particular leaders. Their presence raised doubts about the federalists' entire conception of a virtuous, elite few leading the less sophisticated many. As the singling out of Washington for hypocrisy suggests, this was a critique of the actual founders, not just their ideological limits, as potent and pointed as any seen in our times, but in a political language that fit theirs.

The point that the framers should be held to the highest contemporary standard and might be found wanting was perhaps best made by those whose patriot credentials went back as far as Washington's. The antifederalist Hugh Hughes, a currier, tanner, and former deputy quartermaster general originally from the Quaker stronghold of Upper Merion Township, west of Philadelphia, was a political veteran of the Sons of Liberty in New York. His brother, John Hughes, had accepted the job of stamp distributor in 1765 on Benjamin Franklin's recommendation, only to face an angry anti–Stamp Act mob. In 1787, Hugh Hughes was employed as a tutor by John Lansing, a key figure in New York antifederalism and a delegate to the state ratification convention. Hugh Hughes knew something about surfaces, hypocrisy, and irony in politics. He saw the likes of Franklin, Hamilton, and Madison as politicians, not demigods, and he put his wisdom and experience on full display in a series called "A Countryman from Dutchess County."

Hughes pulled no punches. The convention delegates were "Enemies to the Rights of Mankind," a fact evident in their renewal of the African slave trade. This action alone would ruin the new nation's reputation. Apparently, Samuel Johnson's famous remark of 1775 about "yelps for liberty" coming from the drivers of slaves still rang in Hughes's ears: "Will it not be said, that the greatest Sticklers for Liberty, are its worst Enemies?" Worst of all, in Hughes's mind, was Benjamin Franklin, head of the Pennsylvania Abolition Society, for helping "frame a Constitution which evidently has a Tendency not only to enslave all those whom it ought to protect; but avowedly encourages" the enslavement of others. As soon as it was adopted, politicians like Franklin would say it was "called for by the people," Hughes observed, though really it was nothing but a specious deal between North and South: "If you will permit us to import Africans as Slaves, we will consent that you may export

Americans, as soldiers." The supremacy and treaty clauses meant that Americans, like Hessians during the war, could be "detached and transported to the West or East-indies."

Hughes's next essays went after Franklin and John Dickinson, the Pennsylvania figures he knew so well, as hypocrites. By January, he had taken aim at the militaristic and imperial designs of some of the founders, particularly Alexander Hamilton, whose "junto" he had been observing closely in New York, and who had recently published, in the same newspaper, the early *Federalist* essays on the need for a stronger government to project American power abroad. Hughes insisted that the American Revolution ought to have ensured more than the promise to march "500 or 1000 miles to quell an insurrection of such emigrants as are proposed by the new constitution, to be introduced for one and twenty years. No, nor of butchering the natives, that a few great speculators and landholders may engross all the best soil for a song."[23]

After his anti-Hamilton piece, Hughes shifted emphasis to the three-fifths clause in a satirical essay in the voice of a federalist. Slaves were three-fifths represented, explained this pseudo-Publius, as compensation for their enslavement. Hamilton's agreement to this "right of virtual representation" was a "daring insult" to freeholders that revealed how little he cared about ordinary people.[24]

These arguments were powerfully and extensively reinforced by the publication, beginning in late December, of the convention delegate Luther Martin's *Genuine Information*, an exposé that he had originally presented as a speech to the Maryland legislature in late November. Martin revealed the diversity of sentiment within the convention on national supremacy, representation, and the slave trade. He also echoed earlier published denunciations of deal making and euphemism with regard to slavery. Slavery was "inconsistent with the genius of republicanism," Martin insisted. "When our own liberties were at stake, we *warmly* felt for the common rights of man." There was no logical reason why a government bound to protect the states against invasions and insurrections could not regulate the migration of slaves. Martin remained a states' righter, but he still could not comprehend why the government could not be strong in interstate matters like slavery while leaving the states to themselves on domestic issues. The inconsistency suggested that within the structure of the Constitution, crucial liberties had been sacrificed, and not for the common good. The *New York Journal*, a few days before Hughes's anti-Publius essay, quoted Martin as saying that small states "would be as absolutely slaves as any negro is to his masters." Martin had time to think about how he would pose his public critique of the Constitution, and he chose not just to denounce the slave trade, or slave representation, but to link the issue to his other criticisms, probably because he perceived a receptive audience for the linkage beyond Maryland.[25]

So often the story of the antifederalists, when it gets told at all, is relayed as much less than the dialogue with the framers that it actually became. The fact that Hugh Hughes responded directly and repeatedly to the *Federalist* as it appeared serially in New York newspapers suggests a need to see federalist arguments in favor of the Constitution, in turn, as a strategy in response to critics like Centinel, Brutus, Hughes, and Martin. The federalist strategy of silence regarding slavery did not completely work; by the time Alexander Hamilton, John Jay, and later James Madison began composing their great defenses of the Constitution, the document had already been criticized from multiple angles—hence the need to write federalist papers at all. Just as significantly, many aspects of the antifederalist case against the Constitution, such as representation, the standing army, national supremacy, vagueness, and the deal-making nature of the document, had been connected vividly to the particular place of slavery in the plan.

How did federalists respond?

They had the easiest time with the slave-trade provisions, which seemed the most open to interpretation. The states could still prohibit their own citizens from engaging in the slave trade, insisted Noah Webster. Gradual emancipation was best for blacks and whites anyway, he wrote, and others agreed. Abolitionists like Benjamin Rush, and James Wilson in the Pennsylvania convention, argued that the intention and result of Article I, Section 9 would be the end of the slave trade in 1808, which would amount to nothing less than the beginning of the end of American slavery, in the same gradual mode that it had been enacted in several northern states. A federalist in the Massachusetts convention stated that slavery had "received a mortal wound, and will die of a consumption." Madison echoed this claim with typical precision in Federalist 38, where he mentioned that the Articles of Confederation had permitted slave

Federalist arguments for Convention [handwritten margin note]

importation forever (by not mentioning it). In Federalist 42, he wrote that under the Constitution the slave trade "may terminate forever in these states" in two decades, "a great point gained in favor of humanity." He implied the federal government would certainly discourage the trade through the permissible ten-dollar import tax, and also stressed that the "great majority" of states had ended the trade anyway. Europeans had not done so much.[26]

Madison chose not to mention that in the Philadelphia convention, he, like Wilson, had stated clearly that twenty years of slave trading could also do profound "damage," and might even secure the future of slavery. Similarly, Tench Coxe, a Pennsylvania Abolition Society member who had collaborated with Franklin in squelching the society's petition, wrote one anonymous essay, the "American Citizen," for a Pennsylvania audience in which he depicted the slave-trade clause as wholly antislavery, even as a concession by Southerners. Later, in another anonymous piece, Coxe assured the Virginia convention that Northerners would protect Southerners from invasions and slave rebellions, and referred to the three-fifths ratio as a concession to the South.[27]

The arguments of Wilson, Coxe, and Madison reveal the emerging federalist strategy where it concerned slavery and the Constitution. In the short run, in response to northern antislavery antifederalism, they sought to claim the high ground, and even antislavery intent. They said different things, with different emphases, to different audiences. They stepped up their identification of themselves with civic service and depicted their opponents as self-interested, clueless provincials. (Benjamin Franklin would contribute an essay comparing antifederalists to the Jews of the book of Exodus, who, having escaped from Egyptian slavery only to deny Moses's God-given laws, asked whether they ought to "suffer ourselves to be made Slaves by Moses.") Federalists also began to admit that specific compromises had been made. They defended the spirit of compromise as a good in itself, and, to northern and upper-southern audiences, blamed the Deep South delegates for insisting upon clauses they could not defend.[28]

The Federalist partook of all these strategies, reflecting the deep engagement of its authors with both the Constitution's framing and the battle for ratification in the states. For reasons of temperament and timing, Madison wrote the essays of the series that bore directly and indirectly on slavery. In the largest sense, the very nature of the *Federalist* essays, in aiming for abstraction and balance, tended away from the kinds of inflammatory and morally based arguments that Centinel, Brutus, Benjamin Gale, Hugh Hughes, and others had made against the Constitution. Herbert J. Storing noted that antifederalists "were less easily persuaded that questions of politics can be freed from questions of conscience," and that observation holds especially true for the Constitution's greatest architect and defender, who believed that religion ought to be kept out of politics, and that appeals to conscience had no place either. *The Federalist* contains Madison's further attempts to make sense of and defend slavery's place in what the convention had produced, in light of moral, and often class-based, attacks on the system he had helped build but did not feel responsible for in every detail.[29]

Madison's first attempt to present the big picture, in the famous tenth Federalist, follows the general strategy of not bringing up slavery where it need not be mentioned—and he wrote it relatively early, in November, when the major antifederalist essayists were only just building slavery into their overall critique. He did not depict slavery as a source of the factionalism or majoritarian tyranny that a larger republic could help counteract. In the words of one sympathetic commentator, he "withheld" his earlier assertion, in the convention, that wealthy slaveholders typified the dangers of both minority and majority rule. If slavery epitomized the "local prejudices" and "schemes of injustice" endemic to state politics, one would not know it from Publius. Instead, slavery is rationalized, rather than criticized, as another economic and geographical interest.[30]

The division of subjects into their analytical parts in *The Federalist Papers* enables Madison to reassert control over the subject of slavery and to dissolve the connections antifederalists made. Countering the antifederalist argument that everything is connected, Madison insists on deconstructing everything separately and from multiple perspectives. It is not so much that he did not see the links between slavery and the structure of government as that he preferred at this time, for political reasons, to demonstrate the virtues of a dispassionate, analytical mindset. The ability and willingness to do so, even to describe the opposition's arguments in the process, became evidence of "candor," reason, and civility. Because slavery played different roles at different points in his arguments, as in the Constitution itself, he could deal with slavery selectively and effectively, if defensively.[31]

Federalist 42, for example, posited the slave-trade clause as antislavery. It then proceeded to call the antifederalist attempt to interpret the clause as "a criminal toleration of an illicit practice," or as so vague as to allow for a ban or tax on European immigration, as an object lesson in the lack of equanimity "some" showed in criticizing the Constitution. The very next essay, Federalist 43, defends the insurrections clause in a similar way, but with no reference to the likelihood that permitting the slave trade for twenty years or more could increase the chances of slave rebellion. Any number of possible combinations of majorities and minorities, citizens and noncitizens, might join, possibly with foreign aid, in rebellions. "I take no notice," he added, while taking very careful notice, "of an unhappy species of population abounding in some of the States, who, during the calm of regular government, are sunk below the level of men; but who, in the tempestuous scenes of civil violence, may emerge into the human character and give a superiority of strength to any party with which they may associate themselves." Antislavery sentiments are fashioned into reasons why the states need a federal government powerful enough to serve as "umpires" and reasonable enough to adjudicate because "not heated by the local flame." Readers could be forgiven for being unsure whether Publius really saw the insurrections clause as security for slaveholders or rather as the charter of an antiwar tribunal.[32]

These passages on slavery, culminating in Federalist 54, preserve an antislavery pose while allowing for the Constitution's proslavery results. When Madison wrote the numbers of *The Federalist* that deal with the design of the federal government, no southern state had yet ratified; nor had Massachusetts. Madison still needed to defend against antifederalist attacks without offending either Virginians or people in the Deep South.

Writing Federalist 54 for a New York audience within three weeks of the appearance of Hugh Hughes's attack on Publius for accepting the three-fifths clause, Madison displays an uncharacteristic anxiety with his use of the double negative: "It is not contended that the number of people in each State ought not to be the standard for regulating the proportion of those who are to represent the people of each State." The subject was simply fraught with difficulty, because a different principle had led to an agreement that taxes, too, should be based on population. Numbers were simply the best and most practical representation of wealth.[33]

The problem lay in how to think about slaves. If all agreed that slaves were sources of wealth like other people, "does it follow . . . that slaves ought to be included in the numerical rule of representation?" They should be counted as property, but not as members of the polity to be represented. "This is the objection, as I understand it, stated in its full force," Madison writes, ignoring the further articulation of the dangers involved in slave representation that had been contributed by northern antifederalists. His task, rather, was "to be equally candid in stating the reasoning which may be offered on the opposite side."

Madison then performs a remarkable act of ventriloquism, giving over the bulk of this essay to the arguments that "might" be given "by one of our southern brethren." In the South, under the laws, slaves are in fact both persons and property. The Constitution, then, rather than illegitimately creating a federal ratio for slave representation where none existed in the states themselves, correctly reproduces their actual social condition in the states in which they live. In leading with this argument rather than with the northern apology offered by Rufus King and James Wilson that the federal ratio had been "the language of America" since (merely) 1783, Madison had his eyes, as always, on the bigger prize. The example of the three-fifths clause actually showed how respectful the framers had been of precedent and the laws of the states. If anything was unsatisfying about three-fifths, the states were to blame.[34]

Besides, Madison's Southerner continued, if slaves were considered only property and taxed accordingly, it would be not only unfair but more unjust than the laws of slavery, which by contrast admitted that slaves had some rights as persons. Yes, they did not vote in the states, but why should nonvoters be represented in the federal government? Madison again does not reach first for the most obvious argument: that many nonvoters—women, children—came under the census and the rule of personhood, being represented only virtually. Instead, he again makes a federalist virtue out of the status quo. Each state had its own rules for who could vote in elections, and it would be impossible, if not tyrannical, to impose a single rule on the national system of representation. The Southerners had agreed nevertheless to count three-fifths rather than 100 percent of slaves: "All that they ask is that equal moderation be shown on the other side. Let the case of the slaves be considered, as it is in truth a peculiar one. Let the compromising expedient of the Constitution be mutually adopted which regards them as inhabitants, but as debased by servitude below the equal level of free inhabitants; which regards the *slave* as divested of two fifths of the *man*," argues the reasonable, conservative, but not proslavery Southerner.

Having posed the three-fifths clause as both reasonable and a compromise, Madison reached for the brass ring, all the way back to his lasting concern with the protection of property in the wake of the states' "luxuriancy of legislation." If a crucial responsibility of government lay in the protection of property, shouldn't property be represented in the democratic branch, since it was not being represented in the Senate, where the states had succeeded in gaining equal representation? Madison's remarkable ability to make theoretical lemonade out of politics' lemons was once again on display, fashioning another Mansfieldian moment, when the politics of slavery inspires those not necessarily devoted to the issue of slavery to reach for a clarification that recasts statecraft in significant ways. Wealth would be protected but justly limited in its power by this system of representation. In a precise inverse of the multiplier effect foreseen by the antifederalists, in which the corruption of representation by slavery would spoil the entire government and turn them into slaves, Madison posits a future in which slave representation helps to preserve all property, and saves government from the democratic enthusiasms of people like the Shaysites and Hugh Hughes.

The essay creates as many filtration devices as the federal government Publius defends. After allying slave representation with the most conservative arguments in his arsenal, Madison has Publius step back from the southern mask. Lest we think that the government is in fact a creation of planters and northern conservatives (as the antifederalists were arguing), he distances himself from the result, and again displays moderation and rationality in agreeing to it despite the other objections he hasn't addressed:

> Such is the reasoning which an advocate for the Southern interests might imploy on this subject; and although it may appear to be a little strained in some points, yet on the whole, I must confess that it fully reconciles me to the scale of representation which the Convention have established.

Madison then saves for last a new, procedural side benefit of the compromise. Joining taxation and representation (and, he implied, including some but not all slaves) would encourage an accurate census, upon which the entire system of representation would depend. North and South, in the end, could be manipulated into an equitable science of politics.

These singular breaks in the voice of Publius, the avowals and disavowals of "southern" arguments, as well as the reassertions of reason and candor, suggest just how potent a threat the discussion of slavery posed to ratification—not to mention how significant Madison's role was as a maker of the "masks of the law" that enabled Americans of 1787 to nationalize and constitutionalize slavery without feeling implicated. Hugh Hughes noticed the profoundly legalistic dimension of Madison's reasoning immediately, and published his final "Countryman" essay on February 14 in response to Federalist 54, which had appeared two days before. "The Federalist, as he terms himself, or Publius, puts me in mind of some of the gentlemen of the long robe, when hard pushed, in a bad cause, with a rich client. They frequently say a great deal, which does not apply; but yet, if it will not convince the judge or jury, may, perhaps, help to make them forget some part of the evidence—embarrass their opponent, and make the audience stare, besides increasing the practice."[35]

How did such lawyering play out in Virginia? Madison certainly found much need for his practice. His friends begged him to come, and he left New York for Virginia as the state geared up for its convention in May. The largest state had perhaps the most diversity of opinion with respect to slavery. While emancipation schemes had not, and would not, succeed in Virginia, much conventional wisdom still deplored the existence of the institution. George Mason had been the first to accuse the convention of making an illicit sectional deal that came out wrongly on slavery, but his protests made a Virginian kind of sense, which he amplified in later statements. The slave trade was wrong, he argued, but Virginian property and power had been bargained away for national supremacy as well as for Yankee and Carolinian interests. In response, the Connecticut dealers Oliver Ellsworth and Roger Sherman stepped up their attacks in anonymous essays on Mason's own hypocrisy, echoed by Virginia federalists. Nevertheless, antifederalism gained strength in Virginia from the particular nature of the great compromises between the Deep South and New England, which left the Virginians wondering where they stood in the union.

Before the convention, Westerners in Kentucky (still part of Virginia) issued revised versions of the Constitution that struck out the slave-trade clause and, in one case, the three-fifths clause as well. One writer in Lexington made all the main arguments voiced earlier by Gale, the Hampshire dissenters, and Hughes: the vagueness of the slavery clauses, American moral guilt over slavery, the "radically woven into" and "essential" nature of slavery in the Constitution, and the implication that such a frame of government could, "when there shall remain no more black people," allow for the "enslave[ment of] others, white as yourselves."[36]

Eastern Virginia federalists ignored this critique, perhaps because they were also hearing objections from those who thought slave property insufficiently guarded by the new constitution. By the time of the convention in June, the spellbinding two-time former governor Patrick Henry had apparently decided that the best tactic on the part of antifederalists in Virginia would be to split the difference over slavery as Mason had, but with an emphasis more on the risk that slavery might be legislated by outsiders than on the evils of slavery and the slave trade. Henry took up a full quarter of the floor time at the convention, but no one complained. His reworking of the great compromises was every bit as compelling (and partial) as Madison's, and it forced Madison himself into yet another round of argumentation, as well as some new compromises.

Henry himself had corresponded with abolitionists and believed that slavery was wrong. Yet he was the kind of great debater who had little compunction about being inconsistent, for he could always explain his way out of any seeming inconsistency by appealing to some higher principle. *"Give me liberty or give me death"*: he'd been doing so for a quarter century. In September 1774, on the second day of the First Continental Congress's meetings, Henry had weighed in for proportional voting in the Congress on the basis of just such a higher principle—nationalism. According to John Adams, he had said that slaves did not need to be counted, even though counting them would benefit his colony: "I am not a Virginian, but an American." In the 1788 debate, the higher principle was local autonomy, and the encapsulation less lofty: *"They'll take your niggers from you!"*[37]

More than anyone else in the debates, Henry perceived the Mansfieldian dimension of the new constitution: a government with expansive powers, with control over taxation, armed forces, and the economy, could not but govern slavery. He saw a Leviathan in the making, and found in the ambiguities about slavery an ideal way to illustrate the potentially unlimited threat to state sovereignty. What was to keep the federal government from finding ways around the Constitution's silences and seeming discouragements to antislavery legislation?

After federalists like the former dissenter Edmund Randolph argued that the need for defense against invaders, shown during the Revolutionary War, made it absolutely necessary for the state to ratify, Henry asked pointedly the same question some northern antifederalists had asked about conscription, but in a proslavery key. What would prevent quotas of troops from being drafted during any war according to the federal ratio, so that white Virginians had to pay and serve more on account of their slaves? The question was expertly designed to resonate in the wake of Virginia's wartime controversies over which white Virginians would serve in the Revolution, who would pay taxes in lieu of service, and the effects of enlistments and taxes on property in slaves. Moreover, the Continental Congress had asked for southern slaves to be armed: "May Congress not say, that every black man must fight?" Still worse, what would keep a Congress dominated by Northerners from refusing to defend the state from a slave rebellion? Henry even described the restriction on the Congress's power to end the slave trade before 1808 as proof of the government's expansive powers in every other article.[38]

There could be only one explanation for the lack of specific provisions to protect slave property, and Henry said it scared him. "He feared its omission was done with design. They might lay such heavy taxes on slaves, as would amount to emancipation." The mode of taxation, and of determining population for representation, was ultimately left to the Congress. The very fact that Americans, including Henry, detested slavery would tempt its statesmen to find some way to combine its destruction with some other public good. Where New England antifederalists had seen in the power of slaveholders in the federal government a risk to their own liberty and property, Henry saw a lack of power and a risk to slavery and property itself. The northern majority "have not the ties of sympathy and fellow-feeling" with Virginians. Because slavery remained a "local matter," so should government.[39]

On the spot, Madison denied that anyone in the Philadelphia convention had ever contemplated emancipation. He echoed federalist arguments for the Constitution's protection of slavery. This time, he defended the slave-trade compromise as neither emancipationist nor proslavery but simply as the best that could be had thanks to those in the Deep South who accused Virginians of wanting to become suppliers of slaves. Slavery was safer than under the Articles because the Constitution would protect property and because the great compromises were perfectly well understood by all the real players (if not provincials like Henry).

In the end, Patrick Henry and George Mason did not win over enough votes, and Virginia ratified, 89 to 79. But the deliberations led Madison to sign on to Mason's version of a recommended bill of rights that would protect individual liberties (rather than Henry's list that would protect state powers). Given that a similar set of events had occurred in Massachusetts, and the fact that federalists in New Hampshire had deliberately stalled to see if their large neighbor to the south would ratify, it is well worth considering whether the debate on the slavery issue actually made possible the antifederalists' great contribution to the Republic: the drafting and quick adoption of the first ten amendments, led by Madison in the first federal Congress.

The bargaining power that slavery contributed to the

antifederalist cause would certainly help explain the initial presence and curious disappearance of slavery at the contentious New York ratification convention, getting under way in mid-June while New Hampshire and Virginia continued their deliberations.

In April, Albany antifederalists were still exploring, and stressing, how the links between slavery, taxation, and representation corrupted the Constitution and made likely the "rule of the rich." On the second day of the convention, after the delegates agreed to his proposal to proceed clause by clause, Melancton Smith rehearsed his attack on apportionment, the three-fifths clause, and the freedom of a Congress elected through the federal ratio to change the number of representatives as it saw fit. Wicked slaveholders would have more votes, enabling them to control the inadequately represented majority. For Smith, the Revolutionary maxims still applied: "He who is controlled by another is a slave; and that government which is directed by the will of any one or a few, or any number less than is the will of the community, is a government for slaves."[40]

Alexander Hamilton rose to respond. He would speak with "candor" and resolve these matters. To understand the Constitution, he told the delegates, whose number—fifty-seven—approximated the Philadelphia convention, one needed to know what had happened behind closed doors in Philadelphia. Taking the local leaders he had so often derided into his confidence, he explained that the country was divided into "navigating" and "non-navigating" states, which really amounted to the North and the South. These delegates split over commercial regulation, while the small states wanted equality in the legislature. The result was a compromise in which "it was necessary that all parties should be indulged."[41]

Hamilton's description of the convention's work, and especially the parts Smith had objected to, shows that he had read his Madison. He defended the Constitution on the basis of compromise, mutual interest, and the conservative theory of representation:

> The regulation complained of was one result of the spirit of accommodation, which governed the Convention; and without this indulgence, no union could possibly have been formed. But, Sir, considering some peculiar advantages which we derive from them, it is entirely just that they should be gratified. The Southern States possess certain staples, tobacco, rice indigo &c. which must be capital objects in treaties of commerce with foreign nations; and the advantage which they necessarily procure in these treaties, will be felt throughout all the States.

The plan was also just, locally as well as nationally, because the New York Constitution rightly represented property as well as persons. It, too, denied the vote to "a great number of people." The problem with the antifederalist critique of the three-fifths clause, Hamilton argued, lay not only in being unrealistic about geopolitics and economic interests. It was also too democratic for New York.

After Hamilton's speech, which George Clinton called "a second edition of Publius," New York antifederalists said surprisingly little about slavery. Melancton Smith pronounced himself "confident" that Hamilton's defense of Article I, Section 2 "might easily be refuted, yet I am persuaded we must yield this point, in accommodation to the southern states." John Lansing, Hugh Hughes's patron, agreed. Smith kept fighting, however, on the democracy question. Perhaps he was happy enough to have outed Hamilton on representation: the convention delegates who served with Hamilton proceeded to testify to his less-than-democratic statements in Philadelphia. Probably the New York delegates felt time slipping away, as ratification occurred by close votes in the ninth and tenth states of New Hampshire and Virginia on June 21 and June 27. They angled for amendments they could achieve, rather than deals they could not undo.

Lansing provided a clue in one of his convention speeches. Hamilton had admitted in responding to Smith that material interests were at stake in the making of the Constitution. Why had he subsequently started talking about how enlightened congressmen, including those from different sections, would be (in Hamilton's words) "constantly assimilating, 'till they embrace each other, and assume the same complexion"? Were differences real and permanent, or temporary? Was it all just words? By bringing up slavery and democracy, and by relating the two issues, the antifederalists had forced the great Publius to admit that practical talk of particular interests and idealistic appeals to a national identity coexisted uneasily. Mixed and matched, nationalism and complicated compromises could turn into a shell game, a cover for a radical shift in power. Once admitted, though, interests could be brokered, and better representation could be demanded.[42]

The New York antifederalists, in short, achieved as much as they could achieve in late June without further recourse to the slavery issue, at a time when it seemed likely that some union would exist with the three-fifths clause. That they reached an accommodation with the federalists does not make them hypocrites or insincere about slavery: it makes them good politicians, and at least as worthy of our respect as Hamilton and Madison. And like good politicians, they did attempt to sneak their antislavery politics back into their proposed amendments to the Constitution. Lansing's proposed Declaration of Rights included a ban on direct taxes or excises on American manufacturers, to match the South's ban on export taxes. It also denied the federal government the right to order the militia out of the state for more than six weeks without permission of the legislature.[43] Patrick Henry would have been appalled.

Lansing's sons' tutor, Hugh Hughes, may not have been satisfied, but he had certainly been heard. "Will a Majority of the Great Body of the People of the United States contentedly consent to support a Government founded in Usurpation & Fraud, relative to us, and Violence and Rapine relative to others?" the irrepressible Hughes had asked, in a letter to a Connecticut antifederalist in April.[44] The answer would be yes—if their initial protests resulted in concessions like the Bill of Rights.

The antifederalist use of slavery was doomed as an antislavery movement, or moment, by its variability: the critiques offered up by George Mason, Hugh Hughes, Patrick Henry, and the Hampshire dissenters, when brought together, were neither uniform nor consistent. By contrast, the federalists, who so praised consensus, actually seem to have benefited from the federalism of the ratification process: it allowed them to defend the Constitution as proslavery in some states and as antislavery in others. It is easy to forget that for the antifederalists, this diversity among communities was the point. States had their own ways of doing things on matters of real importance, and the people ought to be able to determine the fate of institutions like slavery, and the place of slavery in their constitutional design, according to their own ideals.

Yet there was more to antislavery antifederalism than localism. Hugh Hughes's response to Madison reminds us of one important effect of the Revolutionary generation's encounters with the politics of slavery: a renewed sense among some politically aware Americans that morality, and ideas, could not be compromised without great risk. Antislavery survived the post-Revolutionary backlash epitomized by the Constitution because some Americans refused to believe that the Constitution, or even America, was the ultimate source of their cherished ideals. Some standard outside the nation, one that did not require a benediction from the founding fathers, ought to be the source of legitimacy, a polestar in making political judgments. The religiously inspired abolitionists of the nineteenth century had little choice but to stress God's law after they had been marginalized by the political system. Nevertheless, abolition's own origins did lie before the Revolution and the American nation, in convictions that pointed to human equality and international brotherhood. Hugh Hughes's insistence that this language remained more important than prior agreements about the three-fifths clause, or deals struck by great men using their reason in Philadelphia, puts him squarely in an American countertradition that goes back to the seventeenth century—and, fortunately, forward to our own time.[45]

Epilogue: Whose Constitution?
Toward Civil War

In 1788, federalists gathered to celebrate state ratifications of the Constitution in some of the most impressive parades North America had ever seen. With statesmen and artisans marching with banners and floats, they often succeeded in making the Constitution appear to be the will of the entire American people. In their orations, toasts, and reportage on these grand events, the Constitution's compromises on slavery go almost completely unmentioned. At the July 4, 1788, festivities in New Haven, Connecticut, one toast wished "a perpetual quietus to paper money, tender laws, and African slavery," but the orator Simeon Baldwin leavened his condemnation of the "shocking" survival of slavery in the United States with praise for "the candour and philanthropy of the southern states, that they consented to that liberal clause in our new constitution evidently calculated to abolish a slavery upon which they calculated their riches."[1] Even in this rare mention, the proslavery aspects of the Constitution are strikingly absent. With respect to slavery, the federalists had fashioned a silence, not a consensus—or at most a consensus to be silent.

There is almost no evidence as to what African Americans thought about the great compromises or the Grand Federal Processions in 1787 and 1788.[2] Perhaps the entire episode seemed unimportant compared with what had happened—and almost happened—in 1772, 1775, and 1781. Nevertheless, on July 4, 1788, a group of "black Inhabitants" in Providence, Rhode Island, adopted the increasingly popular practice of celebrating the Fourth of July and, that year, the ratification of the Constitution. They sent their list of toasts in to a local newspaper, *The United States Chronicle.*

There can be no doubt that they conceived of their festivity as a political act. Celebration of the Constitution was controversial, even risky, in Rhode Island, though less so in the commercial hub of Providence. A thousand antifederalists from Providence's rural outskirts also gathered on the Fourth to prevent what they felt was an illegitimate planned celebration of ratification in the public square (Rhode Island had not ratified). According to federalist reports, the planned celebration took place anyway, with five thousand to six thousand people in attendance, though with toasts modified so as to emphasize national independence rather than the Constitution.

For this very reason—because people were watching—the group we know only as the black inhabitants seized the opportunity, and put on the first publicized self-consciously alternative African American celebration-cum-protest. They gathered because they were "pleased with the prospect of a stop being put to the trade to Africa in our Fellow-Creatures, by the Adoption of the Federal Constitution," and the toasts they published focused on peace, on economy, and on slavery.

1. The Nine States that have adopted the Federal Constitution.
2. May the Natives of Africa enjoy their natural Privileges unmolested.
3. May the Freedom of our unfortunate Countrymen (who are wearing the Chains of Bondage in different Parts of the World) be restored to them.
4. May the Event we this Day celebrate enable our Employers to pay us in hard Cash for our Labour.
5. The Merchants and others who take the Lead in recommending Restoration of Equity and Peace.
6. His Excellency General Washington.
7. The Humane Society of Philadelphia.
8. Hon. John Brown, Esq.
9. May Unity prevail throughout all Nations.[3]

The Providence celebrants refused to choose between claiming a right to celebrate as "inhabitants" and making clear their bond to their "countrymen" in chains. They refused to pretend they were not interested in local economic issues and the currency controversy, even to the point of equating good merchant behavior with the peace that Africans the world over deserved. They suggested a moral and political equivalency between the Revolution's greatest hero and the abolitionists in another city.

And, having redrawn the political map to include the world as well as the nation, they raised their glass to the prominent federalist who was also Providence's best-known international slave trader and critic of antislavery.

The black revelers of Providence were no fools. They knew that the Constitution requires of us what the philosopher Antonio Gramsci called the pessimism of the intellect and the optimism of the will. Like many of the antifederalists, they "began to claim the Constitution as their own . . . in effect to make a new constitution through interpretation."[4] The ensuing battles over interpretation shaped the particular order and disorder of American politics, and American abolitionism, too.

Such fundamental differences in interpretation may have ultimately raised the stakes of the conflict over slavery so high as to make another revolution, another civil war, conceivable. Certainly it proved tempting, in a two-party system, for partisans to play the race card despite the widely shared agreement to be silent about slavery. But it was more than temptation in the not-so-short run. It was the return of the Mansfieldian moment, for slavery could not ultimately be detached from the issues of economy and governance that had made slavery so controversial during a revolution about taxation and representation. Consequently, the politics, as well as the economics, of slavery shaped the very conceptions of personhood, property rights, and sex roles during the coming century. What politics repressed with gag rules, or turned into the grand opera of newer, greater compromises in 1819 and 1850, popular culture turned into the music of everyday life. The first blackface minstrel songs took their cues from satires that mocked African American political festivities like the one held in Providence in 1788.[5]

America did become an empire, which meant only more to fight for. When Lincoln and the Republicans arrived on the scene with a tightly woven conception of a way of life at stake in the unconstitutional spread of slavery, the constitutional politics of slavery had become politics itself. Antislavery politicians finally achieved the clarity that the South Carolina convention delegates had brought with them to Philadelphia but that the three-fifths clause, and the official silences, had so carefully muddled. Nothing could be disentangled from slavery.

That is why, in accepting the vice presidency of the Confederacy, Lincoln's onetime friend and fellow Whig congressman Alexander Stephens declared the South's new republic to be dedicated to the defense of African slavery as God's will. It is why the Confederate Constitution mimicked the Constitution of 1787, with the exception of explicit protections for slavery, as well as the autonomy of states.[6] To compromise once again in 1861, either side would have had to give up not just slavery, or antislavery, but also its constitution: its written political order. In this sense, slavery did not itself cause the Civil War. Slavery's Constitution did.

A NOTE ON SOURCES

NOTES

ACKNOWLEDGMENTS

INDEX

A Note on Sources

All studies of the Constitution's creation begin with Max Farrand's *Records of the Federal Convention of 1787*, 4 vols. (rev. ed., 1937), along with James H. Hutson's bicentennial *Supplement to Max Farrand's "Records of the Federal Convention of 1787"* (1987). At least as important, but only just beginning to be mined by scholars of the era, is *The Documentary History of the Ratification of the Constitution*, 22 vols. (1976–), the ongoing project begun by Merrill Jensen and continuing under the direction of John P. Kaminski, Gaspare Saladino, Richard Leffler, and Charles Schoenleber. The *Documentary History* gives access to the breadth and depth of the debate over the Constitution. My sense that there was more to be said about slavery and the Constitution came from perusing their expertly edited volumes as well as two accessible collections that derive from their work: Bernard Bailyn, ed., *The Debate over the Constitution*, 2 vols. (1987); and John P. Kaminski, ed., *A Necessary Evil? Slavery and the Debate over the Constitution* (1995). Some of the material in the *Documentary History* is available on their Web site, www.wisconsinhistory.org/ratification. Farrand's volumes, as well as *Journals of the Continental Congress, 1774–1789*, edited by Worthington Chauncey Ford (1904–37), and the modern *Letters of Delegates to Congress, 1774–1789*, 26 vols., edited by Paul H. Smith (1976–2000), are available on the Library of Congress's American Memory site, www.lcweb2.loc.gov/ammem/amlaw/lawhome.html.

Studies of the Constitution vary not only in their interpretation of the slavery question but in whether they consider it at all. In a penetrating historiographical essay, "The Abolitionist Critique of the United States Constitution," in *Class Conflict, Slavery, and the United States Constitution* (1967), Staughton Lynd noted that many nineteenth-century abolitionists concluded that the Constitution made fatal concessions to slavery (though, as William M. Wiecek describes in *The Sources of Antislavery Constitutionalism in America, 1760–1848* [1977], there was a countertradition, epitomized by Frederick Douglass and Abraham Lincoln, who emphasized the founders' antislavery intentions). Modern scholarship in many ways began, as Lynd observed, with a reaction against the emphasis on slavery by historians like Hermann Von Holst in his *Constitutional and Political History of the United States* (1876). Still-useful volumes like Max Farrand, *The Framing of the Constitution of the United States* (1913), and Charles Warren, *The Making of the Constitution* (1928), argued that slavery was unimportant to the founders' design. Charles Beard concurred in his otherwise very different interpretation, *An Economic Interpretation of the Constitution of the United States* (1913). This line of analysis persisted in later landmark studies like Clinton Rossiter's vigorous and insightful *1787: The Grand Convention* (1966). By the time of Gordon S. Wood's *Creation of the American Republic, 1776–1787* (1967), still the standard study of political ideology during the period, it had become so much a matter of common sense to so many that, to Wood, the issue of slavery did not even need to be mentioned at all. A quarter century later, in Wood's *The Radicalism of the American Revolution* (1991), slavery still merited only a brief, dismissive rebuttal to those who do not see the American Revolution as the fount of "all our current egalitarian thinking."

Some of the older studies of the Constitutional Convention, such as Rossiter's *1787* and Carl Van Doren's *Great Rehearsal* (1948), actually did a better job explaining the place of slavery in the creation of the Constitution. In recent popular treatments, the title usually gives away the interpretation: the more celebratory the account, the less reckoning with slavery. Lively accounts giving minimal treatment to slavery include Catherine Drinker Bowen, *Miracle at Philadelphia* (1966), and Carol Berkin, *A Brilliant Solution* (2002). Recent accounts of the convention that do give significant consideration to the slavery issue include Christopher Collier and James Lincoln Collier, *Decision in Philadelphia* (1986), and David O. Stewart, *The Summer of 1787* (2005).

The downplaying of slavery is also evident in the subtle and learned recent studies of constitutional ideas, and of James Madison in particular, by Jack N. Rakove. See his *Original Meanings: Politics and Ideas in the Making of the Constitution* (1996) and subsequent essays, including "Constitutional Problematics, Circa 1787," in John Ferrejohn et al., eds., *Constitutional Culture and Democratic Rule* (2001); "Thinking Like a Constitution," *Journal of the Early Republic* 24 (Summer 2004); "Confederation and Constitution," in Michael Grossberg and Christopher Tomlins, eds., *The Cambridge History of Law in America, Vol. I* (2008). For a different, equally fascinating interpretation of Madison that is even more dismissive of the significance of slavery, see Lance Banning, *The Sacred Fire of Liberty: James Madison and the Founding of the Federal Republic* (1995).

Of works that do consider slavery and the making of the Constitution explicitly, those taking a middle ground on the question of the Constitution's anti- or proslavery nature include Don E. Fehrenbacher, *The Slaveholding Republic* (2002). Building on his earlier studies, Fehrenbacher argued for the Constitution's neutrality and ambiguity; the proslavery aspects, he believed, mushroomed as a result of later events and implementations, which are the focus of his study. Howard A. Ohline's "Republicanism and Slavery: Origins of the Three-Fifths Clause in the United States Constitution," *William and Mary Quarterly*, 3rd Ser., 28 (Oct. 1971), 563–84, practically opened up the subject with its careful use of sources and its nuanced argument for the unintentional but deeply structured logic of the apportionment non-compromise. Donald L. Robinson's *Slavery in the Structure of American Politics, 1765–1820* (1971) is a neglected classic. More celebrated, but also still repaying careful study for their nuances and careful research, are the acknowledged classics by Winthrop Jordan, *White Over Black: American Attitudes Toward the Negro, 1550–1812* (1967), and David Brion Davis, *The Problem of Slavery in the Age of Revolution, 1770–1823* (1975). William W. Freehling argued for the founders' broad antislavery in an influential 1972 *American Historical Review* essay, "The Founding Fathers and Slavery," but has modified his position in the revised version, "The Founding Fathers, Conditional Antislavery, and the Nonradicalism of the American Revolution," which can be found in his stellar collection, *The Reintegration of American History* (1994).

Staughton Lynd, *Class Conflict, Slavery, and the United States Constitution*, describes a compromise with proslavery results, while always keeping us conscious of the effects of abolitionist thought and politics and indeed the larger sweep of American history. The book will be reissued by Cambridge University Press with a new afterword by Robin Einhorn in 2010. William Wiecek's contribution in *The Sources of Antislavery Constitutionalism in America* is augmented by two bicentennial essays in which he made a careful case for the proslavery dimensions of the Constitution: "The Witch at the Christening: Slavery and the Constitution's Origins," in Leonard W. Levy and Dennis J. Mahoney, eds., *The Framing and Ratification of the Constitution* (1987), 167–84; and " 'The Blessings of Liberty': Slavery in the American Constitutional Order," in Robert A. Goldwin and Art Kaufman, eds., *Slavery and Its Consequences: The Constitution, Equality, and Race* (1988), 23–44. Alfred W. Blumrosen and Ruth G. Blumrosen, *Slave Nation: How Slavery United the Colonies and Sparked the American Revolution* (2005), builds on these foundations and includes chapters on the Constitution; it is especially notable for its emphasis on the Mansfield decision and its tracing of the legal issues back to the 1760s and 1770s.

What the above works have in common is the theme of a compromise with proslavery results. During the 1970s and 1980s, John Hope Franklin and his students Paul Finkelman and A. Leon Higginbotham Jr. made the case for a basically proslavery constitution. They were assisted by the Supreme Court justice Thurgood Marshall in a widely reported and subsequently published talk. See John Hope Franklin, "The Moral Legacy of the Founding Fathers" (1975), in his *Race and History: Selected Essays, 1938–1988* (1988); Raymond T. Diamond, "No Call to Glory: Thurgood Marshall's Thesis on the Intent of a Proslavery Constitution," *Vanderbilt Law Review* 42 (1989), 93–131; A. Leon Higginbotham Jr., *Shades of Freedom: Racial Politics and the Presumptions of the American Legal Process* (1996). Finkelman's "Slavery and the Constitutional Convention: Making a Covenant with Death" appeared first in Richard R. Beeman et al., eds., *Beyond Confederation* (1987), and later in Finkelman's influential collection of essays, *Slavery and the Founders: Race and Liberty in the Age of Jefferson* (1996; rev. ed., 2001). Finkelman's most recent thoughts on the subject appear in his articles "The Founders and Slavery: Little Ventured, Little Gained," *Yale Journal of Law and the Humanities* 13 (2001), 413–48, and "The Root of the Problem: How the Proslavery Constitution Shaped American Race Relations," *Barry Law Review* 4 (2003), 1–19. For critical responses to the proslavery constitution thesis, see W. B. Allen and Herbert J. Storing's essays in Goldwin and Kaufman, *Slavery and Its Consequences*. Mark A. Graber, *Dred Scott and the Problem of Constitutional Evil* (2006), agrees on the overwhelmingly proslavery nature of the Constitution. For a narrative rendering that focuses on the convention, see Lawrence Goldstone, *Dark Bargain: Slavery, Profits, and the Struggle for the Constitution* (2005).

Recent studies of the Constitution and of Madison coming from legal studies and political theory have been more willing than leading historians of the republicanism school to admit to the significance of slavery to the founding. See Richard K. Matthews, *If Men Were Angels: James Madison and the Heartless Empire of Reason* (1994); Akhil Reed Amar, *America's Constitution: A Biography* (2006); and David Brian Robertson, *The Constitution and America's Destiny* (2005). J. David Greenstone paid close attention to the implications of the slavery question in American political thought, beginning with Jefferson and Adams, in *The Lincoln Persuasion: Remaking American Liberalism* (1993). Some sophisticated studies of the nature of the Constitution have made a connection between the Constitution's silences and its treatment of slavery. See especially Jon Leubsdorf, "Deconstructing the Constitution," *Stanford Law Review* 40 (Nov. 1987), 181–97; the historian Jan Lewis's " 'Of Every Age Sex & Condition': The Representation of Women in the Constitution," *Journal of the Early Republic* 15 (1995), 359–87; and Mark Brandon, *Free in the World: American Slavery and Constitutional Failure* (2000). The leading constitutional scholar Sanford Levinson traces his increasing doubts about the Constitution to its treatment of slavery in "It Is Time to Repair the Constitution's Flaws," *Chronicle of Higher Education,* Oct. 13, 2006, an essay that heralded his book *Our Undemocratic Constitution* (2006). Treatments by legal historians stressing the colonial legal background include A. Leon Higginbotham Jr., *In the Matter of Color: Race and the Presumptions of the American Legal Process* (1978), and Jonathan A. Bush, "The British Constitution and the Creation of American Slavery," in Paul Finkelman, ed., *Slavery and the Law* (1997). For the Mansfield decision, see also Steven M. Wise's breathless but informative *Though the Heavens May Fall: The Landmark Trial That Led to the End of Human Slavery* (2005); Christopher Leslie Brown's *Moral Capital: Foundations of British Abolitionism* (2006); and George Van Cleve, "Somerset's Case and Its Antecedents in Imperial Perspective," *Law and History Review* 24 (2006), 601–45.

There have been few studies of slavery and the ratification debates, but see James Oakes, " 'The Compromising Expedient': Justifying a Proslavery Constitution," *Cardozo Law Review* 17 (1995–96), 2023–56; Kenneth Morgan, "Slavery and the Debate over the Ratification of the United States Constitution," *Slavery and Abolition* 22 (Dec. 2001), 40–65; and John Craig Hammond, " 'We Are to Be Reduced to the Level of Slaves': Planters, Taxes, Aristocrats, and Massachusetts Antifederalists, 1787–1788," *Historical Journal of Massachusetts* (2003), 172–98. Matthew Mason's *Slavery and Politics in the Early American Republic* (2005) and "Slavery and the Founding," *History Compass* 4/5 (2005), 943–55, stress the utility of the slavery issue as a "weapon" for all sides in the debate over the Constitution. For ratification in the states, see Michael Allen Gillespie and Michael Lienesch, eds., *Ratifying the Constitution* (1989), and Patrick T. Conley and John P. Kaminski, *The Constitution and the States* (1987), as well as the older studies by Jackson Turner Main, *The Antifederalists: Critics of the Constitution* (1961), and Robert Allen Rutland, *The Ordeal of the Constitution* (1966). For the antifederalists' ideas, see Herbert J. Storing, *What the Anti-Federalists Were For* (1981), and Saul Cornell, *The Other Founders: Antifederalism and the Dissenting Tradition in America, 1788–1828* (1999).

Other recent studies of the making of the Constitution illuminate key aspects of the Constitution's formation and have influenced my sense of slavery's relation to its other attributes. On compromise, see Peter B. Knupfer, *The Union as It Is: Constitutional Unionism and Sectional Compromise, 1787–1861* (1991). For sectionalism and politics in the 1780s, see H. James Henderson, *Party Politics in the Continental Congress* (1974); Joseph L. Davis, *Sectionalism in American Politics, 1774–1787* (1977); Peter S. Onuf, *The Origins of the Federal Republic, 1775–1787* (1983); and David C. Hendrickson, *Peace Pact: The Lost World of the American Founding* (2004). For the state-building dimension of federalism, see Max M. Edling, *A Revolution in Favor of Government* (2003). For the issues of taxation and democracy, see the superlative treatments by Woody Holton, *Unruly Americans and the Origins of the Constitution* (2007), and Terry Bouton, *Taming Democracy: The "People," the Founders, and the Troubled Ending of the American Revolution* (2007). Alfred F. Young explores the Constitution's compromises in terms of class and ideology in two landmark essays, "The Mechanics of the Revolution: 'By Hammer and Hand All Arts Do Stand' " and "Conservatives, the Constitution, and the 'Genius of the People' " in his *Liberty Tree: Ordinary People and the American Revolution* (2006). Robin L. Einhorn brilliantly sets the proslavery aspects of the Constitution in a wider institutional and chronological framework in *American Taxation, American Slavery* (2006). How to relate culture and government in this era is considered by Michael Meranze, "Culture and Government," *William and Mary Quarterly*, 3rd ser., 65 (Oct. 2008), and Eric Slauter's forthcoming *The State as a Work of Art: Cultural Origins of the Constitution* (2009). Selective but useful recent overviews of the scholarship on the Constitution appear in Gwenda Morgan, *The Debate on the American Revolution* (2008), Alan Gibson, *Interpreting the Founding* (2006), and Alan Gibson, *Understanding the Founding* (2007).

For a broad perspective on constitutionalism and the British Empire, see Jack P. Greene's *Peripheries and Center* (1986) and his collection of essays, *Negotiated Authorities* (1994), as well as Daniel Hulsebosch, *Constituting Empire: New*

York and the Transformation of Constitutionalism in the Atlantic World, 1664–1830 (2005). John Philip Reid's *Constitutional History of the American Revolution*, 4 vols. (1985–93), dismisses the slavery issue but parses key constitutional questions related to slavery, including taxation, representation, and sovereignty. For the imperial approach to the coming of the Revolution more generally, see Lawrence Henry Gipson's magisterial *The British Empire Before the American Revolution*, 14 vols. (1937–70), as well as Theodore Draper's lucid and evocative *A Struggle for Power: The American Revolution* (1996).

The subject of African Americans and slavery in the Revolutionary era has seen a renaissance of scholarship, which properly began with Benjamin Quarles, *The Negro in the American Revolution* (1961), continued with Sidney Kaplan and Emma Nogrady Kaplan, *The Black Presence in the Era of the American Revolution* (1973; rev. ed., 1987), and reached a crescendo with Sylvia Frey, *Water from the Rock: Black Resistance in a Revolutionary Age* (1991); Peter H. Wood, " 'Liberty Is Sweet': African-American Freedom Struggles in the Years Before White Independence," in Alfred F. Young, ed., *Beyond the American Revolution* (1993); Graham Russell Hodges, *Root and Branch* (1999), on New York; Woody Holton's *Forced Founders* (1999) and Michael McDonnell's *Politics of War* (2006), on Virginia; and Robert Olwell's *Masters, Slaves, and Subjects* (1998), on South Carolina. There are several helpful essays on the topic in John P. Resch and Walter Sergent, eds., *War and Society in the American Revolution* (2007). The trend toward seeing African Americans as key players has recently culminated in Cassandra Pybus, *Epic Journeys of Freedom: Runaway Slaves of the American Revolution and Their Global Quest for Liberty* (2005), and Simon Schama, *Rough Crossings: Britain, the Slaves, and the American Revolution* (2005). Ira Berlin and Gary B. Nash helped pioneer this literature, and Berlin's *Many Thousands Gone* (1998) and *Generations of Captivity* (2004), as well as Nash's *Race and Revolution* (1991), *The Unknown American Revolution* (2004), and *The Forgotten Fifth: African Americans in the Age of Revolution* (2006), synthesize many studies, as will Douglas R. Egerton's *Death or Liberty* (2009).

For the impact of the slavery question on the American revolutionaries, see, in addition to the works by Donald Robinson, Winthrop Jordan, and David Brion Davis cited above, Patricia Bradley, *Slavery, Propaganda, and the American Revolution* (1998), which deals with Boston in the years before 1776; David Waldstreicher, *Runaway America: Benjamin Franklin, Slavery, and the American Revolution* (2004); Henry Wiencek's *An Imperfect God: George Washington, His Slaves, and the Creation of America* (2003); and Robert G. Parkinson's forthcoming study of the Revolutionary War years, *Enemies of the People*. Dickson D. Bruce's *Origins of African American Literature, 1680–1865* (2002) is much broader than its title sounds and particularly strong on the challenge that African American antislavery writing posed. For Jefferson, in addition to the work of Jordan and Davis cited above, see John Chester Miller, *The Wolf by the Ears: Thomas Jefferson and Slavery* (1977); Finkelman's essays on Jefferson in *Slavery and the Founders*; Peter S. Onuf's *Jefferson's Empire: The Language of American Nationhood* (2000) and *The Mind of Thomas Jefferson* (2007); and my introduction to the Bedford Books edition of *Notes on the State of Virginia and Related Documents* (2002). William G. Merkel argues for the significance of Jefferson's antislavery efforts in the 1780s in "Jefferson's Failed Anti-slavery Proviso of 1784 and the Nascence of Free Soil Constitutionalism," *Seton Hall Law Review* 38 (2008), 555–603.

The political dimensions of struggles for emancipation are treated in Arthur Zilversmit, *The First Emancipation* (1967), and in recent studies by Eva Shepard Wolf, *Race and Liberty in the New Nation: Emancipation in Virginia from the Revolution to Nat Turner's Rebellion* (2006), and David N. Gellman, *Emancipating New York: The Politics of Slavery and Freedom, 1777–1827* (2006). Studies of individual emancipators in their local contexts have come into their own in well-written books like Andrew Levy's *First Emancipator: The Forgotten Story of Robert Carter, the Founding Father who Freed His Slaves* (2005) and Charles Rappleye's *Sons of Providence: The Brown Brothers, the Slave Trade, and the American Revolution* (2005).

The intertwined politics of slavery and nationhood that resulted from the Revolution and the Constitution have been treated in many works, including some of those above. For later crises and compromises, see William W. Freehling, *The Road to Disunion*, Volume 1: *Secessionists at Bay, 1776–1854* (1991); Matthew Mason, *Slavery and Politics in the Early American Republic*; and Robert Pierce Forbes, *The Missouri Compromise and Its Aftermath* (2007). Two new works take a cultural approach akin to that pursued here: François Furstenberg, *In the Name of the Father: George Washington's Legacy, Slavery, and the Making of a Nation* (2006); and Elizabeth R. Varon, *Disunion! The Coming of the American Civil War, 1789–1859* (2008).

Notes

Prologue: Meaningful Silences

1. Bernard Bailyn, "The Central Themes of the American Revolution" and "The Ideological Fulfillment of the American Revolution: A Commentary on the Constitution," in *Faces of Revolution* (New York, 1990), 200–68; Gordon S. Wood, *The Radicalism of the American Revolution* (New York, 1991); Jack N. Rakove, *Original Meanings: Politics and Ideas in the Making of the Constitution* (New York, 1996).

2. Bernard Bailyn, *The Ideological Origins of the American Revolution* (Cambridge, Mass., 1967), 232–46; Gordon S. Wood, *The American Revolution* (New York, 2002), 126–29; Gordon S. Wood, "Reading the Founders' Minds," *New York Review of Books,* June 28, 2007, 63.

3. Bernard Bailyn, *On the Teaching and Writing of History* (Hanover, N.H., 1994), 58–60; Bernard Bailyn, *Context in History* (Melbourne, Australia, 1995), 15–18.

4. Thomas G. West, *Vindicating the Founders* (Lanham, Md., 1997), 26–28, 168–69; Jean M. Yarbrough, *American Virtues: Thomas Jefferson on the Character of a Free People* (Lawrence, Kans., 1998), 9–10.

5. Paul Finkelman, *Slavery and the Founders* (Armonk, N.Y., 1996), 2; A. Leon Higginbotham Jr., *Shades of Freedom: Racial Politics and the Presumptions of the American Legal Process* (New York, 1996), 68–71; Lawrence Goldstone, *Dark Bargain: Slavery, Profits, and the Struggle for the Constitution* (New York, 2005).

6. Staughton Lynd, *Class Conflict, Slavery, and the United States Constitution* (Indi-

anapolis, 1967), 3–21, 135–213; William M. Wiecek, "The Witch at the Christening: Slavery and the Constitution's Origins," in Leonard W. Levy and Dennis J. Mahoney, eds., *The Framing and Ratification of the Constitution* (New York, 1987), 167–84; William M. Wiecek, " 'The Blessings of Liberty': Slavery in the American Constitutional Order," in Robert A. Goldwin and Art Kaufman, eds., *Slavery and Its Consequences: The Constitution, Equality, and Race* (Washington, D.C., 1988), 23–44; Alfred W. Blumrosen and Ruth G. Blumrosen, *Slave Nation: How Slavery United the Colonies and Sparked the American Revolution* (Naperville, Ill., 2005); Christopher Collier and James Lincoln Collier, *Decision in Philadelphia: The Constitutional Convention of 1787* (New York, 1986); Pinckney in John P. Kaminski, ed., *A Necessary Evil? Slavery and the Debate over the Constitution* (Madison, Wis., 1995), 170.

1: The Mansfieldian Moment

1. A search of the online version of Early American Imprints, a database of works printed in America before 1800, yielded no printings of the song in the colonies. "An American Parody on 'Rule Britannia' " appeared in Pinckney's *Virginia Gazette* on Dec. 1, 1774, and can be heard on the CD *In Freedom We're Born: Songs from the American Revolution* (WCSD-124), produced by the Colonial Williamsburg Foundation.

2. Joshua Gee, *The Trade and Navigation of Great-Britain Considered* (London, 1729); James Logan, "Of the State of the British Plantations in America: A Memorial," in Joseph E. Johnson, ed., "A Quaker Imperialist's View of the British Colonies in America," *Pennsylvania Magazine of History and Biography* 60 (1936), 128; Benjamin Franklin, "Observations Concerning the Increase of Mankind," in *The Papers of Benjamin Franklin*, ed. Leonard W. Labaree et al. (New Haven, Conn., 1959–), vol. 4, 225–34.

3. John Oldmixon, *The British Empire in America*, 2 vols. (London, 1741; repr., New York, 1969), xviii, xxviii; Malachy Postlethwayt, *The African Trade, the Great Pillar and Support of the British Plantation Trade in America* (London, 1745), 4–6, quoted in Lawrence Henry Gipson, *The British Empire Before the American Revolution* (New York, 1960), vol. 2, 268; James Abercromby, "An Examination of the Acts of Parliament Relative to the Trade of the American Colonies" (1752), in Jack P. Greene, Charles F. Mullett, and Edward C. Papenfuse, eds., *Magna Charta for America* (Philadelphia, 1986), 218–19.

4. Adams quoted in Frederick B. Wiener, "The Rhode Island Merchants and the Sugar Act," *New England Quarterly* 3 (1930), 464; Gipson, *British Empire Before the American Revolution* (New York, 1961), vol. 10, 124–25.

5. Charles William Taussig, *Rum, Romance, and Rebellion* (New York, 1928), 31.

6. Stephen Hopkins, "An Essay on the Trade of the Northern Colonies," *Newport Mercury*, Feb. 6 and 13, 1764; Stephen Hopkins, *The Rights of Colonies Examined* (Providence, 1764), in Merrill Jensen, ed., *Tracts of the American Revolution, 1763–1776* (Indianapolis, 1967), 5, 9–11, 43.

7. James Otis, *The Rights of the British Colonies Asserted and Proved* (1764), in Bernard Bailyn, ed., *Pamphlets of the American Revolution* (Cambridge, Mass., 1965), vol. 1, 435–36, 439–40.

8. R. C. Simmons and P. D. G. Thomas, eds., *Proceedings and Debates of the British Parliaments Respecting North America* (Millwood, N.Y., 1982–87), vol. 2, 88–89, 130; Lawrence Henry Gipson, *The Coming of the Revolution, 1763–1775* (New York, 1954), 113.

9. Benjamin Franklin, "Subjects of Subjects," in *Papers of Benjamin Franklin*, vol. 15, 36–38; William Knox, *The Claim of the Colonies to an Exemption from Internal Taxes Imposed by Authority of Parliament Examined* (London, 1765), 5–6; William Knox, *Three Tracts Respecting the Conversion and Instruction of Negro Slaves in the Colonies* (London, 1768); *The Constitutional Right of the Legislature of Great Britain, to Tax the British Colonies in America, Impartially Stated* (London, 1768), vii, 9.

10. Frank Moore, ed., *Songs and Ballads of the American Revolution* (1855; repr., Port Washington, N.Y., 1964), 37.

11. Thomas Jefferson, *Notes on the State of Virginia with Related Documents*, ed. David Waldstreicher (Boston, 2002), 11–12, 43–44.

12. J. G. A. Pocock, *The Machiavellian Moment: Florentine Political Thought and the Atlantic Republican Tradition* (1975; rev. ed., Princeton, N.J., 2003), viii, 577.

13. Henry to Pleasants, Jan. 18, 1773, in Roger A. Bruns, ed., *Am I Not a Man and a Brother: The Antislavery Crusade of Revolutionary America, 1688–1788* (1977; repr., New York, 1980), 222.

14. Samuel Seabury, *A View of the Controversy Between Great Britain and Her Colonies* (London, 1774); "The Final Hearing Before the Privy Council Committee on Plantation Affairs," in *Papers of Benjamin Franklin*, vol. 21, 48–49; Samuel Johnson, *Taxation No Tyranny*, 3rd ed. (London, 1775), 36, 64, 79, 85.

15. *Resistance No Rebellion: In Answer to Doctor Johnson's "Taxation No Tyranny"*

(London, 1775), 5, 28; *An Answer to a Pamphlet, Entitled "Taxation No Tyranny"* (London, 1775), 61; Edmund Burke, "Speech in Support of Resolutions for Conciliation with the American Colonies," in Edmund Burke, *On the American Revolution: Selected Speeches and Letters,* ed. Elliott R. Barkan (New York, 1965), 83, 85, 91–92.

16. Franklin to Jonathan Shipley, July 7, 1775, in *Letters of Delegates to Congress, 1774–1789,* ed. Paul H. Smith (Washington, D.C., 1976–2000), vol. 1, 605–7; Woody Holton, *Forced Founders: Indians, Debtors, Slaves, and the Making of the American Revolution in Virginia* (Chapel Hill, N.C., 1999), 153–54; Robert Olwell, *Masters, Slaves, and Subjects: The Culture of Power in the South Carolina Low Country* (Ithaca, N.Y., 1998), 230; Hooper to Joseph Trumbull, March 13, 1776, in *Letters of Delegates to Congress,* vol. 3, 374.

17. Burke, "Speech in Support of Resolutions for Conciliation," 92.

18. Thomas Jefferson, *Autobiography,* in *Thomas Jefferson: Writings,* ed. Merrill Peterson (New York, 1984), 21–22. For a further, technical discussion of the drafting and editing of these passages of the Declaration, see my *Runaway America: Benjamin Franklin, Slavery, and the American Revolution* (New York, 2004), 213–14, 286–88nn7–8.

19. Gregory J. W. Urwin, "When Freedom Wore a Red Coat: How Cornwallis's 1781 Campaign Threatened the Revolution in Virginia," *Army History* (Summer 2008), 6–23.

20. L. H. Butterfield et al., eds., *Diary and Autobiography of John Adams* (Cambridge, Mass., 1962), vol. 2, 182–83; William Whipple to Josiah Bartlett, April 27, 1779, in *Letters of Delegates to Congress,* vol. 12, 398; Henry Wiencek, *An Imperfect God: George Washington, His Slaves, and the Creation of America* (New York, 2003), 190; John Shy, introduction to John Resch and Walter Sargent, eds., *War and Society in the American Revolution* (DeKalb, Ill., 2007), 16; for an argument that the British army and navy probably deserve the prize for integration, see Simon Schama, *Rough Crossings: Britain, the Slaves, and the American Revolution* (London, 2005), 123.

21. The Continental Congress's first order of business—deciding how its delegates would vote—forced the slavery question onto the table on the Congress's second day of meeting. In arguing for proportional representation instead of one vote per state, Patrick Henry insisted that state boundaries did not matter to the patriot movement: "We are in a state of nature." The issue was one of democracy—and nationhood: "The Distinctions between Virginians, Pennsylvanians, New Yorkers and New Englanders, are no more. I am not a Virginian, but an American. Slaves are to be thrown out

of the Question, and if the freemen are to be represented according to their numbers, I am satisfied." Delegates from Rhode Island and Virginia (Benjamin Harrison) proceeded to insist that states had to have equal votes (and the Congress quickly voted that day to keep their deliberations secret). Thomas Lynch of South Carolina argued that property ought to be considered in representation. *Letters of Delegates to Congress,* vol. 1, 28, 30.

22. Worthington Chauncey Ford, ed., *Journals of the Continental Congress* (Washington, D.C., 1904–37), vol. 6, 1079, 1099–1100; Butterfield et al., *Diary and Autobiography of John Adams,* vol. 2, 245–48.

23. Patricia Bradley, *Slavery, Propaganda, and the American Revolution* (Oxford, Miss., 1998).

24. Jefferson, *Autobiography,* 25–26.

25. *Journals of the Continental Congress, 1774–1789,* vol. 6, 1080; Robin L. Einhorn, *American Taxation, American Slavery* (Chicago, 2006), 123.

26. *Journals of the Continental Congress,* vol. 25, 948–49; also John P. Kaminski, ed., *A Necessary Evil? Slavery and the Debate over the Constitution* (Madison, Wis., 1995), 22.

27. Alfred W. Blumrosen and Ruth G. Blumrosen, *Slave Nation: How Slavery United the Colonies and Sparked the American Revolution* (Naperville, Ill., 2005), 152–53; the Articles of Confederation, Nov. 15, 1777, in Donald S. Lutz, ed., *Colonial Origins of the American Constitution: A Documentary History* (Indianapolis, 1998), 377.

2: The Great Compromises of the Constitutional Convention

1. Benjamin Franklin, *Information to Those Who Would Remove to America* (1784), in *Franklin: Writings,* ed. J. A. Leo LeMay (New York, 1987), 975–83.

2. Thomas Jefferson, *Notes on the State of Virginia with Related Documents,* ed. David Waldstreicher (Boston, 2002); David Brion Davis, *The Problem of Slavery in the Age of Revolution, 1770–1823* (Ithaca, N.Y., 1975), 174; William G. Merkel, "Jefferson's Failed Anti-slavery Proviso of 1784 and the Nascence of Free Soil Constitutionalism," *Seton Hall Law Review* 38 (2008), 555–603.

3. Madison to James Madison Sr., Sept. 8, 1783, in *Letters of Delegates to Congress, 1774–1789,* ed. Paul H. Smith (Washington, D.C., 1976–2000), vol. 20, 627; *The Writings of James Madison,* ed. Galliard Hunt (New York, 1901), vol. 2, 154.

4. Fredrika Teute Schmidt and Barbara Ripel Wilhelm, "Early Proslavery

Petitions in Virginia," *William and Mary Quarterly*, 3rd ser., 30 (January 1973), 138–39, 141, 145.

5. Gordon to John Adams, Sept. 7, 1782, quoted in Joseph L. Davis, *Sectionalism in American Politics, 1774–1787* (Madison, Wis., 1977), 59–60, 63, 67–68.

6. Jefferson to Chastellux, Sept. 2, 1785, in *The Papers of Thomas Jefferson*, ed. Julian P. Boyd et al. (Princeton, N.J., 1950–), vol. 8, 467–69; John Chester Miller, *The Wolf by the Ears: Thomas Jefferson and Slavery* (New York, 1977), 30; Chastellux quoted in Andrew Levy, *The First Emancipator: The Forgotten Story of Robert Carter, the Founding Father Who Freed His Slaves* (New York, 2005), 117.

7. Worthington Chauncey Ford, ed., *Journals of the Continental Congress* (Washington, D.C., 1904–37), vol. 25, 948–49; James Madison to Edmund Randolph, Apr. 8, 1783, in *Letters of Delegates to Congress*, vol. 20, 152–53; Robin L. Einhorn, *American Taxation, American Slavery* (Chicago, 2006), 144.

8. Jefferson to Madison, April 25, 1784, in *Letters of Delegates to Congress*, vol. 21, 545.

9. *Maryland Journal*, July 3, 1786, in John P. Kaminski et al., eds., *The Documentary History of the Ratification of the Constitution*, 22 vols. (Madison, Wis., 1976–), vol. 13, 154.

10. Terry Bouton, *Taming Democracy: "The People," the Founders, and the Troubled Ending of the American Revolution* (New York, 2007), 171; Woody Holton, *Unruly Americans and the Origins of the Constitution* (New York, 2007); Leonard Richards, *Shays's Rebellion: The American Revolution's Final Battle* (Philadelphia, 2002); Ronald P. Formisano, *For the People: American Populist Movements from the Revolution to the 1850s* (Chapel Hill, N.C., 2008), 27–34.

11. Christopher Leslie Brown, *Moral Capital: Foundations of British Abolitionism* (Chapel Hill, N.C., 2006); Kirsten Sword, "Remembering Dinah Nevil" (paper presented at the Atlantic Emancipations conference, McNeil Center for Early American Studies, Philadelphia, April 2008).

12. David Waldstreicher, *Runaway America: Benjamin Franklin, Slavery, and the American Revolution* (New York, 2004), 228–33.

13. David O. Stewart, *The Summer of 1787: The Men Who Invented the Constitution* (New York, 2007), 51; Max Farrand, ed., *The Records of the Federal Convention of 1787*, rev. ed. (New Haven, Conn., 1937), vol. 1, 15–16; James Madison, *Notes of Debates in the Federal Convention of 1787 Reported by James Madison* (1966; repr., New York, 1987).

14. Jefferson to John Adams, Aug. 30, 1787, in Farrand, *Records*, vol. 3, 76; Carl Van Doren, *The Great Rehearsal* (1948; repr., New York, 1965), 36–37; Clin-

ton Rossiter, *1787: The Grand Convention* (New York, 1966), 167–69; George Mason to George Mason Jr., June 1, 1787, in Farrand, *Records*, vol. 3, 32.

15. Farrand, *Records*, vol. 1, 32; William Lee Miller, *The Business of May Next: James Madison and the Founding* (Charlottesville, Va., 1992), 121; Stewart, *Summer of 1787*, 57, 63.

16. Farrand, *Records*, vol. 1, 24, 26–27.

17. Ibid., 31–32; Madison, *Notes*, 35–36.

18. Farrand, *Records*, vol. 1, 135.

19. See, for example, Howard A. Ohline, "Republicanism and Slavery: Origins of the Three-Fifths Clause in the United States Constitution," *William and Mary Quarterly*, 3rd Ser., 28 (Oct. 1971), 573–74; Jack N. Rakove, "The Great Compromise: Ideals, Interests, and the Politics of Constitution Making," *William and Mary Quarterly*, 3rd Ser., 44 (July 1987), 427, 449–50; Jack N. Rakove, "The Madisonian Moment," *University of Chicago Law Review* 55 (1998), 487–89; Gordon S. Wood, *The Presence of the Past: Reflections on the Uses of History* (New York, 2008), 299. Compare David Brian Robertson, *The Constitution and America's Destiny* (New York, 2005), 135; David A. J. Richards, "Revolution and Constitutionalism in America," in Michael Rosenfeld, ed., *Constitutionalism, Identity, Difference, and Legitimacy* (Durham, N.C., 1994), 90.

20. Farrand, *Records*, vol. 1, 146.

21. James H. Hutson, ed., *Supplement to Max Farrand's "The Records of the Federal Convention of 1787"* (New Haven, Conn., 1987), 70.

22. Farrand, *Records*, vol. 1, 193–95, 206; Madison, *Notes*, 98–106; Hutson, *Supplement*, 70.

23. Farrand, *Records*, vol. 1, 318; vol. 4, 25.

24. William Blount to John Gray Blount, June 15, 1787, in Hutson, *Supplement*, 76; see also John Lansing to Philip Schuyler, June 26, 1787, in ibid., 121; Farrand, *Records*, vol. 1, 450–52, 460.

25. Madison, *Notes*, 224–25.

26. Farrand, *Records*, vol. 1, 509, 517.

27. That same evening, Franklin received the petition against the slave trade passed by the Pennsylvania Abolition Society a month earlier. According to the vice president of the Society, Tench Coxe, Franklin decided to let it "lie over for the present." Coxe to Madison, in Farrand, *Records*, vol. 3, 361.

28. Farrand, *Records*, vol. 1, 527, 535, 561–62; Dickinson in Hutson, *Supplement*, 158; Madison, *Notes*, 261, 268, 278–79.

29. Madison, *Notes*, 286.

30. Staughton Lynd, "The Compromise of 1787," in *Class Conflict, Slavery, and the United States Constitution* (Indianapolis, 1967), 185–213. Lynd presents his account of the deal around the Northwest Ordinance and the three-fifths clause as a hypothesis; I present some of his best evidence below, but I do not think the matter need rest on the specific question of whether a specific person can be said to have carried word from New York to Philadelphia. Recent accounts that follow and slightly modify Lynd include Christopher Collier and James Lincoln Collier, *Decision in Philadelphia: The Constitutional Convention of 1787* (New York, 1986), 204–22; Alfred W. Blumrosen and Ruth G. Blumrosen, *Slave Nation: How Slavery United the Colonies and Sparked the American Revolution* (Naperville, Ill., 2005), 193–98, 203–24. For an unconvincing attempt to repudiate Lynd that ignores his best evidence and associates his account with Forrest McDonald's unproven assertion of a deal between Roger Sherman and John Rutledge (only to conclude that the lack of proof "does not mean that such maneuvering did not occur"), see James H. Hutson, "Riddles of the Constitutional Convention," *William and Mary Quarterly*, 3rd ser., 44 (July 1987), 415–18.

31. William Grayson to James Monroe, Aug. 8, 1787, in *Letters of Delegates to Congress*, vol. 24, 353; Edward Coles, "History of the Ordinance of 1787" (June 9, 1856), in Hutson, *Supplement*, 321.

32. Madison, *Notes*, 327, 344.

33. Ibid., 355.

34. Donald L. Robinson, *Slavery in the Structure of American Politics, 1765–1820* (New York, 1971), 218; Stewart, *Summer of 1787*, 163–75.

35. Farrand, *Records*, 143, 168–69; Madison, *Notes*, 390.

36. Madison, *Notes*, 409–10.

37. Jack N. Rakove, *Original Meanings: Politics and Ideas in the Making of the Constitution* (New York, 1996), 86–87; Einhorn, *American Taxation, American Slavery*, 167–68; Madison, *Notes*, 411.

38. Madison, *Notes*, 466–67, 501.

39. Ibid., 502.

40. Rakove, *Original Meanings*, 87.

41. Madison, *Notes*, 502.

42. Ibid., 503–4, 506–7.

43. As Gary B. Nash now does. Nash, *The Forgotten Fifth: African Americans in the Age of Revolution* (Cambridge, Mass., 2006), 79–85; Madison, *Notes*, 506.

44. Madison, *Notes*, 530–32.

45. Ibid., 547–52; Farrand, *Records*, vol. 2, 446.
46. Farrand, *Records*, vol. 2, 459; Madison, *Notes*, 610, 633, 648.
47. Farrand, *Records*, vol. 2, 631–33, 636–40; vol. 3, 367.
48. Gordon S. Wood, *The Creation of the American Republic, 1776–1787* (Chapel Hill, N.C., 1967), 626.
49. For the notion of a Madisonian moment, see Rakove, "Madisonian Moment" and *Original Meanings*, 35–56.
50. Joseph J. Ellis, *American Creation: Triumphs and Tragedies at the Founding of the Republic* (New York, 2007), 10.
51. This makes slavery the "leading case in point" for the essentially "conservative" dimensions of the Constitution and the Revolution. Rossiter, *1787*, 270; Richard B. Morris, *The American Revolution Reconsidered* (New York, 1967), 75.
52. Madison, *Notes*, 650–51, 653–54.
53. Ellis, *American Creation*, 237. Ellis sees this dynamic as a Virginian development and blames it on Madison and Jefferson, whereas I see it as quintessentially Revolutionary and far more characteristic of Franklin, New Englanders, and people from the Deep South. No founder published as much about slavery before 1787 as Jefferson; Madison brought slavery before the convention and, while he wanted it to "go away," never thought it could be made to go away without being talked about. Virginians like Mason, Jefferson, and Madison mediated the slavery question because of their geography and their openness to it during the late Revolutionary period.
54. Madison, *Notes*, 659; Henry Wiencek, *An Imperfect God: George Washington, His Slaves, and the Creation of America* (New York, 2003), 264–75.

3: Protesting and Ratifying Slavery's Constitution

1. Diego de Gardoqui to Conde de Floridablanca, Dec. 6, 1787, in John P. Kaminski et al., eds., *The Documentary History of the Ratification of the Constitution* (Madison, Wis., 1976–), vol. 8, 205 (hereafter *DHRC*); Louis-Guillaume Otto to Comte de Montmorin, Nov. 26, 1787, in ibid., vol. 14, 229.
2. John K. Alexander, *The Selling of the Constitutional Convention: A History of News Coverage* (Madison, Wis., 1990).
3. Lester H. Cohen, "The Myth of Consensus and the Antifederalists," *Proteus* 4 (1987), 13–20.

4. Centinel [Samuel Bryan] I, in Bernard Bailyn, ed., *The Debate on the Constitution* (New York, 1987), vol. 1, 62.

5. Cass R. Sunstein, *Legal Reasoning and Political Conflict* (New York, 1996), ix, 4–5, 39.

6. James Oakes, " 'The Compromising Expedient': Justifying a Proslavery Constitution," *Cardozo Law Review* 17 (1995–96), 2023–56; Kenneth Morgan, "Slavery and the Debate over the Ratification of the United States Constitution," *Slavery and Abolition* 22 (Dec. 2001), 40–65.

7. Jonathan Elliot, ed., *The Debates in the Several State Conventions on the Adoption of the Federal Constitution* (Philadelphia, 1836), vol. 4, 283, 338–40; Robert M. Weir, "South Carolina: Slavery and the Structure of the Union," in Michael Allen Gillespie and Michael Lienesch, *Ratifying the Constitution* (Lawrence, Kans., 1989), 201–31; Jerome J. Nadelhaft, "South Carolina: A Conservative Revolution," in Patrick T. Conley and John P. Kaminski, eds., *The Constitution and the States* (Madison, Wis., 1988), 172–78; Rachel N. Klein, *The Unification of a Slave State: The Rise of the Planter Class in the South Carolina Backcountry* (Chapel Hill, N.C., 1990), 165–71.

8. See Matthew Mason's otherwise-excellent *Slavery and Politics in the Early American Republic* (Chapel Hill, N.C., 2006), 27, 32–33.

9. *DHRC*, vol. 4, 32–33.

10. Ibid., vol. 13, 345–46; vol. 14, 103.

11. Ibid., vol. 14, 60–61.

12. Bailyn, *Debate on the Constitution*, vol. 1, 262; *DHRC*, vol. 14, 49; vol. 19, 221, 238.

13. Bailyn, *Debate on the Constitution*, vol. 1, 317–23, 217.

14. Ibid., 449.

15. *DHRC*, vol. 14, 253–54.

16. Ibid., vol. 3, 421–28.

17. Ibid., vol. 4, 69; vol. 7, 1546.

18. Ibid., vol. 4, 67; James Warren, "Republican Federalist," *DHRC*, vol. 5, 834, 845.

19. John Craig Hammond, " 'We Are to Be Reduced to the Level of Slaves': Planters, Taxes, Aristocrats, and Massachusetts Antifederalists, 1787–1788," *Historical Journal of Massachusetts* (2003), 172–98; Leonard Richards, *Shays's Rebellion: The American Revolution's Final Battle* (Philadelphia, 2002); Woody Holton, *Unruly Americans and the Origins of the Constitution* (New York, 2007).

20. Michael Allen Gillespie, "Massachusetts: Creating Consensus," in Gillespie and Lienesch, *Ratifying the Constitution*, 151; Randolph to James Madison, Feb. 29, 1788, cited in John J. Reardon, *Edmund Randolph: A Biography* (New York, 1974), 132.

21. Jack N. Rakove, *Original Meanings: Politics and Ideas in the Making of the Constitution* (New York, 1996), 119.

22. *DHRC*, vol. 7, 1733–42, also excerpted in John P. Kaminski, ed., *A Necessary Evil? Slavery and the Debate over the Constitution* (Madison, Wis., 1995), 100–108, and in Gary B. Nash, *Race and Revolution* (Madison, Wis., 1991), 134–41. The debate continued in the pages of *The Hampshire Gazette*. See *DHRC*, vol. 7, 1745–49; Kaminski, *A Necessary Evil?*, 108–12.

23. *DHRC*, vol. 19, 271, 273–74, 291–92, 427, 496; vol. 20, 636. In December, Hughes had drafted, but not published, an essay titled "Interrogator: To Publius or the Pseudo-Federalist," in which he explicitly accused the author of Federalist 15 of base hypocrisy. How could the Constitution be about extending the authority of the government to its citizens when it clearly claimed authority over the slave trade, which captured and murdered "Africans, who, certainly, are not Citizens of the United States"? *DHRC*, vol. 19, 343.

24. *DHRC*, vol. 20, 659–61, 663–65.

25. "Expositor I," in ibid., vol. 15, 349, 412–14, 434; David N. Gellman, *Emancipating New York: The Politics of Slavery and Freedom, 1777–1827* (Baton Rouge, La., 2006), 86, 250n30.

26. Bailyn, *Debate on the Constitution*, vol. 2, 65, 152; *DHRC*, vol. 2, 462–63; Carl Van Doren, *The Great Rehearsal* (1948; repr., New York, 1965), 250.

27. *DHRC*, vol. 13, 432–33, 539–40; Howard A. Ohline, "Republicanism and Slavery: Origins of the Three-Fifths Clause in the United States Constitution," *William and Mary Quarterly*, 3rd Ser., 28 (Oct. 1971), 582n66.

28. Bailyn, *Debate on the Constitution*, vol. 2, 402–3; Donald L. Robinson, *Slavery in the Structure of American Politics, 1765–1820* (New York, 1971), 45; Peter B. Knupfer, *The Union as It Is: Constitutional Unionism and Sectional Compromise, 1787–1861* (Chapel Hill, N.C., 1991), 32–47.

29. Herbert J. Storing, *What the Anti-Federalists Were For* (Chicago, 1981), 100n20; Richard K. Matthews, *If Men Were Angels: James Madison and the Heartless Empire of Reason* (Lawrence, Kans., 1994), 22, 55.

30. Michael I. Meyerson, *Liberty's Blueprint: How Madison and Hamilton Wrote the Federalist Papers, Defined the Constitution, and Made Democracy Safe for the World*

(New York, 2008), 169–70; Jack N. Rakove, "Constitutional Problematics, Circa 1787," in John Ferejohn, Jack N. Rakove, and Jonathan Riley, eds., *Constitutional Culture and Democratic Rule* (New York, 2001), 62; Matthews, *If Men Were Angels*, 75–77; Robin L. Einhorn, "Patrick Henry's Case Against the Constitution: The Structural Problem with Slavery," *Journal of the Early Republic* 22 (2002), 568.

31. Albert Furtwangler, *The Authority of Publius* (Ithaca, N.Y., 1984), 61–69; Morton White, *Philosophy, "The Federalist," and the Constitution* (New York, 1987), 170; James Madison to Edmund Randolph, Jan. 10, 1788, in Bailyn, *Debate on the Constitution*, vol. 1, 744–46.

32. Clinton Rossiter, ed., *The Federalist Papers* (New York, 1961), 267–70, 276–77.

33. Ibid., 336–37.

34. Ibid., 336–40.

35. Trish Loughran, *The Republic in Print: Print Culture in the Age of U.S. Nation Building, 1770–1870* (New York, 2007), 126–28; John T. Noonan Jr., *Persons and Masks of the Law* (1976; rev. ed., Berkeley, Calif., 2002), 3–64; *DHRC,* vol. 20, 779.

36. *DHRC,* vol. 8, 414–15, 446, 449–51; vol. 9, 774–6.

37. Henry to Robert Pleasants, Jan. 18, 1773, in Roger A. Bruns, ed., *Am I Not a Man and a Brother: The Antislavery Crusade of Revolutionary America, 1688–1788* (1977; repr., New York, 1980), 221–22; L. H. Butterfield et al., eds., *Diary and Autobiography of John Adams* (Cambridge, Mass., 1962), vol. 2, 125; Henry Mayer, *A Son of Thunder: Patrick Henry and the American Republic* (New York, 1986), 433; Einhorn, "Patrick Henry's Case Against the Constitution," 549–55.

38. *DHRC,* vol. 10, 1210, 1305, 1341, 1476. For an outright dismissal of Henry's rhetoric as late and ineffectual, see Lance Banning, *The Sacred Fire of Liberty: James Madison and the Founding of the Federal Republic* (Ithaca, N.Y., 1995), 255, 483n88. For contrary views, see Robert Allen Rutland, *The Ordeal of the Constitution: The Antifederalists and the Ratification Struggle of 1787–1788* (1966; repr., Boston, 1983), 227, 248; and Einhorn, "Patrick Henry's Case Against the Constitution."

39. *DHRC,* vol. 10, 1476–77.

40. Ibid., vol. 21, 1409; vol. 22, 1716, 1719.

41. Ibid., vol. 22, 1727. Since at least late May, Hamilton had been telling antifederalist colleagues that if New York did not adopt the Constitution, the

result might be a division of the northern and southern states. Abraham Yates to John Lansing, May 28, 1788, Abraham Yates Papers, New York Public Library.

42. *DHRC,* vol. 22, 1728, 1748, 1798, 1807.

43. Ibid., 1850, 1871, 2126.

44. Hughes to Ephraim Kirby, April 3, 1788, in ibid., vol. 20, 890–91.

45. For this tradition, see Staughton Lynd, *The Intellectual Origins of American Radicalism* (New York, 1968).

Epilogue: Whose Constitution? Toward Civil War

1. *Connecticut Courant,* July 14, 1788; Simeon Baldwin, *An Oration Pronounced Before the Citizens of New Haven, July 4th, 1788* (New Haven, Conn., 1788), 15–16. The antislavery portion of the *Oration* is excerpted in John P. Kaminski, ed., *A Necessary Evil? Slavery and the Debate over the Constitution* (Madison, Wis., 1995), 112–13.

2. An essay series in *The American Museum* in 1788, by "Othello," whose identity is unknown, denounced the slave-trade clause explicitly, arguing that the framers could have done better and that the results "will forever diminish the luster of their other proceedings, so highly extolled and so justly distinguished for their intrinsic value." He also suggested a connection between the non-ratification of the Constitution by Rhode Island and its new stringent laws against slave trading. Carter G. Woodson, ed., *Negro Orators and Their Orations* (1925; repr., New York, 1969), 16–19.

3. *Newport Mercury,* July 14, 1788; *Providence Gazette,* July 5, 1788; David Waldstreicher, *In the Midst of Perpetual Fetes: The Making of American Nationalism, 1776–1820* (Chapel Hill, N.C., 1997), 100–102; Kaminski, *A Necessary Evil?,* 114.

4. Mark Brandon, *Free in the World: American Slavery and Constitutional Failure* (Princeton, N.J., 1998), 45; see also Saul Cornell, *The Other Founders: Anti-Federalism and the Dissenting Tradition in America, 1788–1828* (Chapel Hill, N.C., 1998).

5. Waldstreicher, *In the Midst of Perpetual Fetes,* 326–44.

6. Alexander Stephens, "The Cornerstone Speech," in Paul Finkelman, ed., *Defending Slavery: Proslavery Thought in the Old South* (Boston, 2003), 92–96.

Acknowledgments

Kate Scott assisted with some of the initial research with great skill and good cheer. Later, audiences at Colgate University and the University of Rochester provided friendly venues and stimulating questions, as did graduate students at Temple University. A very helpful session at the Omohundro Institute of Early American History and Culture and the Early Modern Studies Institute at the Huntington Library in 2007 critiqued a version of the introduction, and I am especially thankful to Toby Ditz, Sarah Knott, Michael Meranze, and Carroll Smith-Rosenberg on that occasion for their advice and encouragement regarding the project as a whole.

Alfred F. Young and Staughton Lynd read a late version of the manuscript, but their roles began much earlier, in correspondence as stimulating as any I've had in years. My colleague Howard Ohline was gracious and encouraging from beginning to end as I walked all over his scholarly territory. I can only hope that after forty years I can sustain the curiosity and gen-

Acknowledgments

erosity they have exemplified. Richard Newman provided an extremely helpful critique of the third chapter. Carl Ackerman, master teacher and master's student, volunteered to read the manuscript and did so with great care and with an eye toward the constructive—I hope I do as well for my students.

Thomas LeBien's sharp wit and good taste shaped this book for the better at every stage. I've said it before and I'll say it again: it's great to have an editor who is both a throwback and cutting-edge. Thanks, Thomas.

Most of all, Jacqueline Robinson's support never wavered, even when, with characteristic wisdom, she told me to be careful what I said about the Constitution.

The book is dedicated to a countryman from Rensselaer County: a great historian and a citizen of the world whose teaching and mentorship have been invaluable.

Index

abolition, abolitionists, 16, 42, 46, 60, 64, 70–71, 103–104, 117, 120, 127, 129, 132, 133, 143, 150–51, 155, 156; *see also* antislavery sentiment

Adams, John, 30, 47, 52, 60, 81, 127, 143

Adams, John Quincy, 123–24

Adams, Samuel, 52, 125

African Americans, 60, 65, 144, 154–57; in Revolutionary War, 9, 44–45, 48–49, 50–51, 52, 57, 60, 62, 96; *see also* slavery, slaves; slave trade

amendment clause, 99, 111, 125

American colonies, 12, 21–46, 125; British blamed for slave trade by, 38, 42, 45, 46, 57, 95–96; early growth of slavery in, 22–23, 27; slave trade temporarily halted in, 6, 36, 45, 53, 95, 127; *see also* Confederation era; Continental Congress

American Indians, 4, 27, 29, 47, 51, 79

American Revolution, 5, 9, 10–15, 22, 30–56, 102, 130, 146, 150, 151, 155; Britain's arming of slaves in, 9, 44–46, 48–49, 51, 57, 60, 62; Constitution criticized for undermining principles of, 111–12, 118–19, 120–21, 122, 126, 146; slavery as metaphor in politics of, 12, 13, 31, 32–38, 42–43; war and military conflict of, 44–45, 48–49, 50–51, 56, 57, 61–62, 94, 96, 144; wartime inflation and debt accumulations in, 15, 62–63, 69, 70

Annapolis Convention, 68–69

antifederalists, 100–101, 103, 110–13, 123–51, 154, 156; anti-ratification essays of, 112–13, 116–21, 126–28, 129–35, 137, 141; on Constitution's overexpansion of federal powers, 111–13, 116, 117, 119

antifederalists (*cont.*)
120–21, 123, 131, 142, 143, 144–
45; Convention deals and compromises criticized by, 108–109, 116,
127, 129–30, 131, 132, 141–42,
144–45, 146, 147, 148–49, 151; federalists' responses to criticisms by,
108, 116–17, 131–41, 142, 146–48
antislavery legislation, 59–61, 66–67
antislavery sentiment, 11–12, 36–46,
50–52, 64, 100, 154–57; in anti-ratification arguments, 100–101,
103, 108–109, 115–23, 126–32,
133, 134, 136, 139, 141, 142–46,
149–50; black role in, 38, 39, 40,
44, 53, 54, 56, 70, 154–57; at Constitutional Convention, 75–77, 80,
85–86, 87, 92, 93–94, 95–97, 103,
135; in Continental Congress,
51, 53, 54, 59–60, 84; in pre-Revolutionary War era, 26–28, 33,
37–39, 42–43; *see also* abolition,
abolitionists; slave rebellions
Arms, Consider, 126–28
Articles of Confederation, 51, 55, 61,
62, 66, 70, 71, 73, 78; slavery protections in, 3, 56, 132–33, 145

Bailyn, Bernard, 10–11, 12, 17
Beard, Charles, 14–15, 17
Bentley, William, 116
Bill of Rights, 145, 149
Blackstone, William, 44
Board of Trade, 23–24, 27, 43
Boston, Mass., 48, 92, 123, 124, 125
British Empire, 21–56, 63, 68, 111;

colonial slave trade imputed to,
38, 42, 45, 46, 57, 95–96; colonies
taxed by, 27, 32–38, 40, 53, 125;
imperial authority imposed by, 24,
26–27, 28–29, 30–31, 34–36, 40,
41, 43, 46, 120, 125; slavery's central role in, 21, 22–23, 24–25, 26–
27, 32; trade and manufacturing
regulations imposed by, 25–27,
30–38; *see also* American colonies;
Great Britain
British West Indies, 25, 27, 29, 32,
33, 39, 48, 49, 62, 63, 68
Brutus (antifederalist writer), 116,
118–19, 132, 134
Bryan, Samuel ("Centinel"), 112–13,
116, 117–18, 134
Burke, Edmund, 43–44, 45–46
Butler, Pierce, 71–72, 77, 78, 86, 93,
98

Canada, 29–30
Cato (antifederalist writer), 116, 119
Chase, Samuel, 51, 53, 54
Clinton, George, 119, 148
Coles, Edward, 87–88
Committee on Detail, 90–95, 98
Compromise of 1850, 88
Confederate Constitution, 157
Confederation era (1776–1787), 4,
15, 49, 50, 63, 66, 79; antislavery
legislation proposed in, 59–61,
66–67; antislavery sentiment in,
46–48, 51, 53, 54, 57–61, 64, 70–
71; Spanish treaty negotiations in,
67–68; state sovereignty vs. cen-

tral governmental powers debated
in, 54, 55–56, 63, 66, 67, 68–70,
73, 75–77, 80, 81; wartime
inflation and debt in, 15, 62–63,
69, 70; widening of North-South
split in, 63–67, 68, 81, 85; *see also*
Constitutional Convention; Continental Congress

Congress, U.S., 3–6, 55, 93, 100,
109, 115, 145; ban on legislating
slave trade in, 3, 7, 9–10, 97–98,
99, 125, 132–33, 136, 144; commerce and taxation powers of, 5–
7, 16, 83, 87, 90–98, 124, 133, 143,
144, 146–47; Constitutional rules
of apportionment for, 3–6, 7, 83,
117–20, 121–22, 144, 146; *see also*
three-fifths clause; in Convention
apportionment debates, 73–90,
91–92, 115, 131, 147; *see also* federal government; legislative
branch

Connecticut, 61, 75, 79, 93, 94, 98,
121–22, 142, 149, 153

Connecticut Compromise, 83

Constitution, U.S., 3–9, 79, 94, 101–
105, 156; ambiguity and "silence"
on slavery in, 3, 6, 9–14, 18–19,
98, 99, 101, 102, 103–104, 113–14,
121, 122, 131, 132, 142, 143;
amendment clause in, 99, 111, 125;
Articles I-IV in, 4–9; Bill of Rights
in, 145, 149; federal government
powers compromised in, 55, 98–
99, 101–102, 114, 116, 131;
fugitive-slave clause in, 8–9, 87, 88,
98, 99, 115; insurrection clause in,

6, 99, 120, 127, 129–30, 131, 133,
136; legislative apportionment
rules in, 3–6, 7, 83, 117–20, 121–
22, 144, 146; *see also* three-fifths
clause; legislative powers of taxation in, 5–6, 7, 83, 87, 90–94, 95,
98, 124, 143, 144; protection of
property in, 8–9, 14–16, 144–45;
slave-trade clauses in, 3, 6–7, 9–
10, 16, 17, 90–95, 97–98, 99, 102,
114, 118, 125, 129–31, 132–33,
136, 142, 144, 145; Southern slave
states empowered and favored in,
4–7, 9, 15–16, 83, 87–88, 89–90,
114, 116–17, 118–20, 121–22, 124,
144–45, 146

Constitutional Convention (1787), 3,
14–18, 19, 51, 69–70, 71–105, 111,
125, 140, 145, 148; allocation of
federal powers debated in, 73, 80,
81, 83, 87, 90–98, 147; antislavery
sentiments raised in, 75–77, 80,
85–86, 87, 92–97, 103, 133, 135;
criticisms on deals and compromises of, 100, 108–109, 116, 127–
28, 129–31, 132, 141–42, 144–45,
146, 147, 148–49; federal powers
limited by compromises in, 55,
90–99, 100, 102, 114, 116, 131; first
great compromise of, 87–90, 91–
92, 116, 133, 146–49, 151, 154; *see
also* three-fifths clause; legislative
representation debated in, 72–90,
91–92, 115, 131, 147; New
England-Deep South alliance at,
16, 90, 93, 94–95, 96, 97–98, 100,
141–42; new territories and

Constitutional Convention (*cont.*) allowance of slavery in, 86, 87–88; pro-federalist and nationalist arguments in, 71, 73, 74, 75–77, 81–83, 91–92, 93, 94, 95–96, 97; pro-state sovereignty delegates in, 77, 79–80, 81–83, 90–96, 100–101; protection of property issue in, 16, 81, 85–87; secrecy and allowance for open discussion at, 16, 71–72, 107, 110, 112; slaveowners' power and influence in, 88, 89–95, 97, 116, 118; slavery issue brokered in compromises at, 16–17, 19, 84, 87–89, 90–95, 97–99, 101–103, 129–31, 145; slave trade in second great compromise at, 90–98, 99, 100, 115, 116, 119, 123, 129–33, 145, 153, 154; small vs. large states at, 75–76, 79–80, 81, 86–87, 146–47; state sovereignty vs. federal government powers in, 73–77, 80, 81–83, 90–97, 102; taxation based on slave population in, 73, 76, 77–79, 83, 84–86, 87, 90–92; taxation of slave trade in, 90–95, 97–98; three-fifths clause in, 73–74, 77–79, 83–86, 87, 90–92, 94, 99; Virginia Plan proposal in, 71, 73–80, 83, 89, 91

Continental army, 15, 48, 50–51, 62, 66, 125

Continental Congress, 3, 15, 38, 46, 50–56, 57, 63, 80, 91, 107, 111, 119, 127, 144; antislavery sentiments and legislation raised in, 51, 53, 54, 59–60, 66–67, 84; new territory slave issues debated in, 59–60, 66–67, 68, 87–88; proportional representation debated in, 73–74, 143; state sovereignty vs. central government debated in, 54, 55–56, 63, 66, 67, 68, 143; taxation debates in, 51–55, 61, 62, 66, 73, 85; three-fifths compromise of, 55, 73–74, 84, 85

Cornwallis, Lord, 49

Coxe, Tench, 133–34

Declaration of Independence, 9, 46–48, 54, 57, 126

Declaratory Act, 34

Delaware, 74, 112

Dickinson, John, 35, 37, 51, 55, 85, 93, 97, 130

Dunmore, Lord, 44

Economic Interpretation of the Constitution of the United States (Beard), 14–15

Ellis, John J., 102–103

Ellsworth, Oliver, 90, 95, 96, 142

emancipation, 51, 52, 104, 125, 132, 141, 144, 145; Northern trend of, 49, 50, 59–61, 70

executive branch, 7, 8, 9, 73, 89

federal government, 14–19, 73, 84, 87, 109, 137, 140; antifederalist view of, 111–13, 116, 119, 120–21, 123, 131, 142, 143, 144–45; Consti

tutional compromises on, 55,
90–99, 101–102, 114, 116, 131;
Continental Congress debates on,
54, 55–56, 63, 66, 67, 68, 143;
Convention debates on allocation
of powers to, 73, 80, 81, 83, 87,
90–98, 147; effect of slavery
clauses on, 80, 117–20, 124, 131,
135, 139, 146; movement for
stronger central powers of, 67, 68–
70, 71, 73, 75–77, 82, 91, 102, 111,
112, 125–26, 130, 131, 136, 143;
protection of property by, 8–9,
14–16, 75, 144–45; slave trade regulation limited in, 3, 9–10, 90–98,
99, 100, 102, 114, 131, 133, 142,
144; *see also specific branches of
government*
Federalist papers, 108, 126, 130, 131,
132–41
federalists, 67, 68–70, 71, 76, 102,
109, 110, 111, 115–17, 120, 121,
123–24, 128–50, 156; ratification
process rushed by, 112, 113;
silence on Constitutional slavery
issues by, 108, 135, 153–54; slave-
trade clauses defended by, 115,
132–33, 135–36, 145; three-fifths
clause defended by, 133, 137–40,
146–48
Field, Samuel, 126–28
Finkelman, Paul, 16
France, 24, 29–30, 32, 57–58, 63, 65,
67, 68, 69, 78; in Revolutionary
War, 48, 62
Franklin, Benjamin, 25–28, 29–30,
44, 47, 53, 54, 57–58, 61, 70–71,

78, 129, 133, 134; in Constitutional Convention debates, 78,
80–81, 82–83, 98, 103–104, 110;
pro-colonial autonomy efforts of,
35–36, 41–43; slavery regulation
called for by, 26–28, 42
fugitive-slave clause, 8–9, 87, 88, 98,
99, 115
fugitive slaves, 38, 39–42; Britain's
wartime recruitment of, 44–46,
49; Mansfield decision and, 39–
42

Gale, Benjamin, 120–22, 126, 134,
142
Gee, Joshua, 25
Georgia, 46, 48, 61, 66, 79, 86, 96,
100, 114, 119
Gerry, Elbridge, 75, 77–78, 79, 97,
100, 101, 103
Gordon, William, 63
Gorham, Nathaniel, 90
Gramsci, Antonio, 156
Grand Committee, 82–84, 87–88
Great Britain, 11, 24, 28–29, 34, 63,
67, 68, 120; antislavery sentiment
and protests in, 39–40, 41–42, 70;
Mansfield decision in, 39–42; in
Revolutionary War, 44–45, 48–
49, 50, 56, 57, 60, 61–62, 96; slavery issue used against American
patriots by, 12, 13, 36, 43; wartime
recruitment of American slaves by,
9, 44–46, 48–49, 51, 57, 60, 62, 96;
see also British Empire
Guadeloupe, 29

Hamilton, Alexander, 10, 74, 75, 76–77, 104, 126, 129, 146–49; *Federalist* papers of, 126, 130, 132
Hancock, John, 111, 125
Harrison, Benjamin, 52, 55
Henry, Patrick, 42, 142–45, 149, 150
Hopkins, Stephen, 25, 32
House of Representatives, U.S., 3–4, 5, 7; Constitutional apportionment rules for, 4–6, 7, 83, 117–20, 121–22, 144–45, 146; *see also* three-fifths clause; proportional representation debates for, 78–79, 83–86, 87, 139–40, 146; *see also* Congress, U.S.
Hughes, Hugh, 120–21, 129–32, 134, 137, 140, 141, 142, 148, 149, 150, 151

insurrections clause, 6, 99, 120, 127, 129–30, 131, 133, 136
Iron Act (1750), 25–26

Jay, John, 67, 68, 132
Jefferson, Thomas, 40, 41, 42, 58–60, 64–67, 69, 72, 95, 100, 110; anti-slavery legislation proposed by, 37–38; anti-slavery statement in early draft of Declaration of Independence by, 46–48, 54; proposed slavery ban in new territories by, 59–60, 66–67
Johnson, Samuel, 43, 129
judiciary branch, 8, 73, 89

Kentucky, 68, 86, 142
King, Rufus, 85, 91, 92, 97, 123, 138
Knox, William, 35–36, 43

Lansing, John, 129, 148–49
legislative branch, 3–7, 73, 89; Convention debates on allocation of powers to, 73, 80, 81, 83, 87, 90–98; proportional representation controversy and, 4–5, 72–90, 91–92, 116, 117–20, 121–22, 124, 131, 132, 137–40, 143, 144, 146–49; *see also* three-fifths clause; Southern power in, 5–7, 77–78, 83–84, 92, 118–22, 144–46; *see also* Congress, U.S.; federal government
Lincoln, Abraham, 157
Logan, James, 25
Lowndes, Rawlins, 115
Lynch, Thomas, 53
Lynd, Staughton, 16

Madison, James, 10, 16, 55, 59, 66, 68–70, 87–88, 129, 143, 147, 149, 150; at Constitutional Convention, 74, 75–77, 80, 81–82, 83–84, 93, 94, 97, 98, 99; *Federalist* papers of, 126, 132–41; in legislative representation debates, 74, 76, 80, 81–82, 83, 84; slave-trade clause and, 97, 98, 132–33, 136, 145; in state sovereignty vs. federal powers debate, 66, 67, 68–70, 75–77, 81–82, 93, 136
Mansfield, Lord, 34, 39–42, 54, 55

Mansfield decision, 39–42, 44, 55
Martin, Luther, 80, 82–83, 93–94, 96, 130–31, 132
Maryland, 68, 78, 80, 82, 96, 98, 111
Mason, George, 72, 93, 95–96, 97, 100, 101, 103, 104, 117, 141–42, 145, 150
Massachusetts, 25, 30, 43, 49, 50, 52, 63, 75, 85, 93, 94, 119; in ratification process, 111, 122–28, 132, 137, 145; Shays's Rebellion in, 69, 92, 111, 123, 124, 125, 126
Maynard, Malachi, 126–28
Missouri Compromise, 88
Molasses Act (1733), 25, 27, 32
Monroe, James, 67
Morris, Gouverneur, 85, 86, 91–92, 97, 103, 104

Neal, John, 122–23
New England, 22, 30–33, 46, 47, 48, 59, 63, 64, 65, 68, 69, 87, 144; Deep South in alliance with, 16, 90, 93, 94–95, 96, 97–98, 100, 141–42
New Hampshire, 61, 66, 97, 150; ratification process in, 122, 123, 145, 146, 148
New Jersey, 67, 79
New Jersey Plan, 79–80
New York, 22, 48, 59, 61, 63, 65, 66, 68, 70, 87, 92, 104, 129, 130, 131, 137, 141, 147; in ratification process, 111, 129, 146–49
North, 17, 30, 49, 52, 86–89, 97, 115– 51; emancipation trend in, 49, 50,

59–61, 70; widening split between South and, 63–67, 68, 81, 85; *see also specific states*
North Carolina, 44, 45, 49, 61, 68, 71, 85, 86, 96, 97, 111, 114
Northwest Ordinance, 87–88, 98
Notes on the State of Virginia (Jefferson), 58–59, 85

Otis, James, 30–31, 33, 35
Otto, Louis-Guillaume, 109–10

Paine, Thomas, 62–63
Parliament, 21, 23–27, 29, 32, 34, 35–36, 41, 43, 124
Paterson, William, 79–80, 84
Pennsylvania, 8, 22, 26, 27, 29, 36, 53, 65, 66, 69–71, 74, 112, 116, 120, 132; gradual emancipation in, 49, 59, 60–61, 70
Pennsylvania Abolition Society, 70, 104, 133
Philadelphia, Pa., 48, 71, 92, 110, 111, 129
Pinckney, Charles, 78, 89, 91, 92, 95, 96, 115
Pinckney, Charles Cotesworth, 16, 79, 95, 96, 97, 98, 103, 104, 115
Pitt, William, 30, 34
Pocock, J.G.A., 40–41
poll taxes, 118, 124, 125
Postlethwayt, Malachy, 27
property rights, 30–31, 32, 41, 59–61, 69, 81, 147; in Constitutional Convention debates, 16, 81, 85–87;

property rights (*cont.*)
  debating definition of slaves as
  property and, 51, 53–54, 138, 139;
  federal government and, 8–9, 14–
  16, 75, 144–45; slavery maintained
  in protection of, 14–16, 18, 31, 35,
  48, 115, 139–40
Publius essays, 126, 130, 131, 132–
  41, 148

Quakers, 42, 70, 120, 122, 129

Randolph, Edmund, 73, 74, 81,
  85–86, 90, 97, 99, 103, 125, 143–
  44
ratification process, 3, 15, 100, 103–
  104, 107–51; of amendments, 99;
  antislavery objections in, 108–109,
  115–23, 126–32, 133, 134, 135,
  136, 139, 141, 142–46, 149–50; cel-
  ebrations and protests after conclusion of, 153–57; slave trade
  clauses criticized in, 114, 115, 116,
  118, 119, 120, 122–23, 126–33,
  135, 136, 141, 142, 144, 145; state-
  by-state voting in, 107, 108, 110–
  11, 137, 148, 153; taxation and
  power issues raised in, 121–22,
  123–25; three-fifths clause debated
  in, 101, 116, 118–20, 121–22, 124–
  25, 130, 132, 133, 137–40, 142,
  146–48, 151; *see also* antifederalists;
  federalists
republican government, 10, 18, 40–
  41, 60, 63, 73, 75, 80, 81; slavery

clauses as corruption of, 117–20,
  131, 139, 146
Republican Party, 157
Rhode Island, 25, 32, 111, 154–57
Robertson, David Brian, 76
Rush, Benjamin, 132
Rutledge, Edward, 54, 55, 115
Rutledge, John, 78, 90, 91, 93, 94–95,
  98, 99, 115

Senate, U.S., 4, 5, 6, 7, 79, 80–83, 84,
  89, 139
Seven Years' War, 29–30, 31, 111
Sharp, Granville, 39, 41–42
Shays's Rebellion, 69, 92, 111, 123,
  124, 125, 126, 140
Sherman, Roger, 75, 79, 91, 92, 95,
  98, 142
slaveowners, 17, 37, 38, 39, 47, 51–56,
  62, 63, 67, 135; Constitution's protection and empowerment of, 4–7,
  9, 15–16, 83, 87–88, 89–90, 114,
  116–17, 118–19, 121, 136, 144–45,
  146; influence and power at Constitutional Convention of, 88,
  89–95, 97, 116, 118; parliamentary
  sovereignty as threat to, 40, 41, 49
slave rebellions, 38, 44, 47, 53, 54, 56,
  94, 144; insurrection clause on, 6,
  99, 120, 127, 129–30, 131, 133, 136
slavery, slaves, 11–12, 14, 21–29, 57,
  69–70, 104, 122, 156; American
  regional differences and vices
  attributed to, 63–65, 81; American
  Revolution escalated by spiraling
  politics of, 43–48, 49; Articles of

Confederation as protecting institution of, 3, 56, 132–33, 145; Beardian scholars theory on, 14–18; Britain's wartime recruitment and arming of, 9, 44–46, 48–49, 51, 57, 60, 62, 96; British Empire and central role of, 21, 22–23, 24–25, 26–27, 32; Constitutional compromises and, 16–17, 19, 84, 87–89, 90–95, 97–98, 101–103, 114, 129–31, 145, 146–47, 153; Constitutional protections of, 3, 6, 7, 8–9, 16, 17, 87, 88, 89–90, 97–99, 101, 102, 104–105, 114, 115, 116–23, 127, 128, 129–33, 136, 138, 141–42, 144, 145, 153–54, 157; Constitution's ambiguity and "silence" on, 3, 6, 9–14, 18–19, 98, 99, 101, 102, 103–104, 113–14, 121, 122, 131, 132, 143; as defined as property, 51, 53–54, 76, 78, 85–86, 98, 138, 139–40, 144; federal government as potentially corrupted by, 80, 117–20, 124, 131, 135, 139, 146; fugitive-slave clause and, 8–9, 87, 88, 98, 99, 115; insurrection suppression clause and, 6, 99, 120, 127, 129–30, 131, 133, 136; in legislative proportional representation controversy, 4–5, 72–90, 91–92, 116, 117–20, 121–22, 124, 137–40, 143, 144, 146–49; Mansfield decision and, 39–42; as metaphor in British politics, 12, 13, 21, 31, 32–38, 42–43; new territories and, 59–60, 66–67, 68, 87–88; as property rights issue, 14–16, 18, 31, 35, 41, 48, 51, 53–54, 59–61, 85–86, 115, 138, 139–40, 144–45; republican government as undermined and corrupted by, 117–20, 124, 135; "republican" scholars theory on Constitutional framing and role of, 11–14, 17, 18–19; resistance and insurrections by, 38, 39, 40, 44, 53, 54, 56, 70, 94; Southern states empowered by clauses on, 5–6, 7, 77–78, 83–84, 85–86, 92, 93, 116, 118–20, 121–22, 124, 144–45, 146; in state sovereignty vs. strong federal government debates, 75–77, 80, 81–82, 94, 102, 143; in taxation debates, 51–55, 61, 62, 73, 76, 77, 79, 83, 84–86, 87, 90–91, 92, 137, 138, 140, 146

slave trade, 32, 56, 84, 104, 125, 154; American colonies in temporary halting of, 6, 37–38, 45, 53, 95, 127; Britain blamed by colonists for creation of, 38, 42, 45, 46, 57, 95–96; Constitutional Convention's compromises on, 90–98, 99, 100, 115, 116, 119, 123, 129–33, 145, 153, 154; federal government's limited power over, 3, 9–10, 90–98, 99, 100, 102, 114, 131, 133, 142, 144; ratification debates objecting to clauses on, 114, 115, 116, 118, 119, 120, 122–23, 126–31, 132–33, 135, 136, 141, 142, 144, 145, 146; state sovereignty in regulation of, 90–98, 99, 132, 143; taxation clauses and debates on, 6–7,

slave trade (*cont.*)
90–95, 97–98, 118, 133, 136, 144, 149; temporary ban on legislation for elimination of, 3, 7, 9–10, 97–98, 99, 125, 132–33, 136, 144
Smith, Melancton, 118, 146, 147, 148
Somerset, James, 39, 55
Somerset v. Steuart (Mansfield decision), 39–42, 44, 55
South, 17, 27, 30, 44, 46–47, 49, 67, 87, 89, 100, 103, 108, 129–30, 133, 134, 137, 140, 148, 157; Britain's invasion of, 44–45, 48–49, 56; in legislative representation debates, 77–79, 82–84, 85, 115, 137–40, 147; New England alliance with, 16, 90, 93, 94–95, 96, 97–98, 100, 141–42; protection of property issue and, 16, 48, 59–61, 85–87, 115, 138, 139–40, 144–45; ratification debates in, 114–15, 141–45; slave rebellion threat and military protection issue in, 6, 94, 144; slavery clauses as empowering states in, 5–6, 7, 77–78, 83–84, 85–86, 92, 93, 116, 118–20, 121–22, 124, 144–45, 146; slave trade clauses put forth by, 90–98, 145
South Carolina, 16, 22, 33, 44, 46, 48, 51, 53, 54, 63, 71, 78, 79, 83, 85, 86, 114–15, 157; in New England Convention alliance, 90–91, 93, 94–95, 96, 97–98, 100, 141–42
Spain, 22, 24, 63, 67–68
Stamp Act, 34, 36, 40, 125, 129
state sovereignty, 50, 63, 79, 84, 131, 135, 138, 157; in arguments opposing Constitution ratification, 111–12, 121–24, 143, 144–45, 150; Constitutional Convention debates on, 73, 75–77, 80, 81–82, 85–86, 93, 96–97; Continental Congress debates on, 54, 55–56, 63, 66, 67, 68, 143; slavery used in support argument for, 80, 144–45; in slave trade regulation, 90–98, 99, 132; strong central government vs., 54, 55–56, 63, 66, 67, 68–70, 73, 75–77, 80, 81–82, 93, 96–97, 102, 109, 111–12, 121–26, 136, 143, 144–45; tax and power issues as entwined with, 73, 75–77, 85–86, 90–95, 96, 121–25, 144; wartime inflation and debt as further incited by, 7, 62–63, 69
Stephens, Alexander, 157
Steuart, Charles, 39
Storing, Herbert J., 134
Sugar Act (1764), 32, 33
Sunstein, Cass, 113

taxation, 9, 32–38, 66, 89, 112, 122, 144, 156; as based on slave population, 51–55, 61, 62, 73, 76, 77, 79, 83, 84–86, 87, 90–91, 92, 137, 138, 140, 146; Congressional powers and, 5–7, 83, 87, 90–95, 97–98, 124, 133, 143, 144; Constitutional Convention debates on, 73, 76, 77–79, 83, 84–86, 87, 90–95, 97–98, 137; Continental Congress debates on, 6, 9, 51–55, 61, 66, 85; ratification debates on issues of

power and, 121–22, 123–25;
Shays's Rebellion and, 69, 92, 111,
123, 124, 125, 140; slave trade
clauses and debates on, 6–7, 90–
95, 97–98, 118, 133, 136, 144, 149;
state sovereignty and, 73, 75–77,
85–86, 90–95, 96, 121–25, 144;
three-fifths compromise and, 4–6,
55, 73–74, 79, 83, 84–86, 87, 90–
92, 94, 118, 137, 138, 140, 146
Tennessee, 86
three-fifths clause, 7, 10, 83–87, 115,
149, 157; Constitutional Convention debates on, 77–79, 83–86, 87,
90–92, 94, 99, 147; critics of, 77–
78, 101, 116, 118–20, 121–22, 124–
25, 130, 132, 137, 142, 146, 147,
149, 151; legislative representation
and, 4–5, 7, 73–74, 77–79, 83–84,
87, 89, 91–92, 116, 118–20, 121–
22, 124, 132, 137–40, 144, 146–49;
Southern states empowered by, 5–
6, 7, 77–78, 83–84, 85–86, 92, 93,
116, 118–20, 121–22, 124, 146;
taxation of states and, 4–6, 55,
73–74, 79, 83, 84–86, 87, 90–92,
94, 118, 137, 138, 140, 146
trade, 23, 28, 29, 53, 54, 146; American postwar issues in reviving of,

62–63, 67–68; imperial regulations imposed on, 25–27, 30–38,
42; state vs. federal divide in regulation of, 16, 67, 68–70, 90–95, 96,
97–98, 146–47; taxes on, 6–7, 32,
63, 90–95, 97–98

Vermont, 49, 60
Virginia, 8, 22, 27, 31, 33, 39, 44, 49,
52, 58–68, 96, 115, 141; in ratification process, 111, 133, 137, 141–45,
146, 148; slave trade regulation
called for in, 37–38, 42, 96
Virginia Plan, 71, 73–80, 83, 89, 91

Warren, James, 124
Washington, George, 16, 48, 50–51,
61, 104, 110, 127, 128, 155
Webster, Noah, 132
Wedderburn, Alexander, 43
Wilson, James, 53–54, 55, 78, 83,
84–85, 90, 92, 97; slavery clauses
defended by, 117, 132, 133–34,
138
Winthrop, James (Agrippa), 119
Wood, Gordon S., 10–11, 12
Woolen Act, 27